Sweetie!

Sweetie!

50 delectable treats

illustrations by
Daniella Germain

hardie grant books
MELBOURNE · LONDON

Contents

Walnut brownie pops

40 lollipop sticks

500 g (1 lb 2 oz) dark chocolate
(70% cocoa solids, melted)

chocolate sprinkles, for coating

walnut brownie

300 g (10½ oz) dark chocolate
(70% cocoa solids), finely chopped

185 g (6½ oz) unsalted butter,
at room temperature

330 g (11¾ oz/1½ cups) caster
(superfine) sugar

45 g (1¾ oz/¼ cup lightly packed)
soft brown sugar

4 eggs, lightly beaten

2 teaspoons natural vanilla extract

150 g (5½ oz/1 cup) plain
(all-purpose) flour

2 tablespoons cocoa powder

100 g (3½ oz/1 cup) walnuts,
finely chopped

To make the brownie, preheat the oven to 175°C (340°F/Gas 3–4). Grease and line a 31 cm x 21 cm x 5 cm (12½ inch x 8¼ inch x 2 inch) cake tin with baking paper. Place the chocolate and butter in the top of a double boiler over medium heat and stir until melted and smooth. Add the sugars and stir until dissolved. Remove from the heat and cool slightly. Add the egg and vanilla extract and stir to combine. Sift the flour and cocoa together into a large bowl, add the chocolate mixture, combine well and stir in the walnuts.

Pour into the tin and bake for 25–30 minutes or until still fudgy and a skewer inserted into the centre comes out with moist crumbs. Cool completely in the tin.

Line 2 baking trays with baking paper. Using a small ice-cream scoop, scoop out balls of brownie onto the trays. Quickly roll each in the palm of your hands to shape into a neat ball. Insert a stick into each ball and refrigerate for 2 hours or until well chilled and firm.

Carefully dip each brownie pop in the melted chocolate and tap the stick on the side of the bowl while slowly spinning to remove excess chocolate. Roll each pop in the sprinkles to coat well. Stand in styrofoam to dry. Serve immediately or store in an airtight container in the refrigerator for 3–4 days.

Makes 40

Lemon cheesecakes
with
blueberry sauce

90 g (3¼ oz) gingersnap biscuits,
   crushed

40 g (1½ oz) unsalted butter, melted

250 g (9 oz/1 cup) cream cheese at
   room temperature

110 g (3¾ oz/½ cup) caster
   (superfine) sugar

1 egg

1½ tablespoons plain (all-purpose)
   flour

1 tablespoon lemon juice

finely grated zest of 1 lemon

150 g (5½ oz/1 cup) fresh blueberries

blueberry sauce

150 g (5½ oz/1 cup) fresh
   blueberries

55 g (2 oz/¼ cup) caster
   (superfine) sugar

3 tablespoons lemon juice

1 tablespoon blueberry jam

Preheat the oven to 150°C (300°F/Gas 2). Line 30 x 30 ml (1 fl oz/⅛ cup) capacity mini-muffin holes with paper cases.

Combine the crushed biscuit and butter in a bowl. Divide between the cases, press down to form an even crust and refrigerate for 15 minutes.

Place the cream cheese and sugar in the bowl of an electric mixer and beat on medium–high speed for 2 minutes. Reduce the speed, add the egg and beat well, scraping down the sides of the bowl as required. Add the flour, lemon juice and zest and combine well.

Transfer the mixture to a large piping bag fitted with a 3 cm (1¼ inch) plain nozzle and pipe into the paper cases, filling them three-quarters full. Top each cheesecake with 2–3 blueberries, slightly pushing them into the mixture. Bake for 15 minutes or until set. Cool in the tins for 5 minutes, then turn out onto wire racks and cool for 30 minutes. Refrigerate for at least 3 hours.

Meanwhile, to make the sauce, place all of the ingredients in a saucepan over low heat and stir gently until the sugar has dissolved and the blueberries release some of their juices. Using a slotted spoon, remove the berries and set aside. Increase the heat to high and cook until the liquid has reduced by one-third.

Pour over the berries, leave to cool completely, then refrigerate until chilled.

To serve, spoon 1 tablespoon of sauce over each cheesecake.

Makes 30

Mint brownie ice-cream sandwiches

1 litre (35 fl oz/4 cups) mint
  chocolate-chip ice-cream

mint brownie

125 g (4½ oz) unsalted butter

125 g (4½ oz) dark chocolate
  (70% cocoa solids), finely
  chopped

110 g (3¾ oz/½ cup) caster
  (superfine) sugar

95 g (3⅓ oz/½ cup lightly packed)
  soft brown sugar

2 eggs

1½ teaspoons natural mint extract

75 g (2¾ oz/½ cup) plain (all-
  purpose) flour, sifted

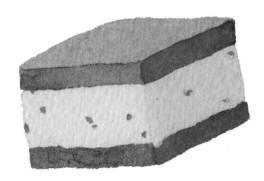

To make the brownie, preheat the oven to 180°C (350°F/Gas 4). Grease and line 2 18 cm x 18 cm (7 inch x 7 inch) cake tins with baking paper. Place the butter and chocolate in the top of a double boiler over medium heat and stir until melted and smooth. Remove from the heat and cool slightly.

Place the sugars, eggs and mint extract in the bowl of an electric mixer and beat on medium speed for 3–5 minutes or until light and combined. Add the chocolate mixture and mix well, scraping down the sides of the bowl as required. Add the flour and beat until just combined. Divide between the tins and bake for 12–14 minutes or until still fudgy and a skewer inserted into the centre comes out with moist crumbs. Cool for 5 minutes in the tins, then remove and cool completely on wire racks.

Place the ice-cream in the refrigerator for 10 minutes or until slightly softened. Line an 18 cm x 18 cm (7 inch x 7 inch) cake tin with plastic wrap, overhanging each side by 10 cm (4 inches). Place one of the brownie slabs in the base, cover with the ice-cream in a thick layer and top with the remaining brownie slab. Cover with plastic wrap and freeze for 4–5 hours or overnight.

To serve, use the overhanging plastic wrap to lift out the brownie sandwich onto a chopping board and slice into 4 cm x 4 cm (1½ inch x 1½ inch) squares.

Makes 16

Chocolate indulgence ice-cream sandwiches

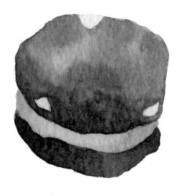

1 litre (35 fl oz/4 cups) chocolate
  ice-cream

225 g (8 oz) dark chocolate
  (70% cocoa solids), melted

chocolate chip cookies

150 g (5½ oz/1 cup) plain
  (all-purpose) flour, plus
  2 tablespoons extra

1 teaspoon baking powder

40 g (1½ oz/⅓ cup) cocoa powder

125 g (4½ oz) unsalted butter,
  at room temperature

165 g (5¾ oz/¾ cup) caster
  (superfine) sugar

1 teaspoon natural vanilla extract

1 egg

120 g (4¼ oz/¾ cup) mini
  milk-chocolate chips

120 g (4¼ oz/¾ cup) mini
  dark-chocolate chips

To make the cookies, preheat the oven to 175°C (340°F/Gas 3–4). Line 2 baking trays with baking paper. Sift together the flour, baking powder and cocoa. Place the butter, sugar and vanilla extract in the bowl of an electric mixer and beat on medium speed for 1–2 minutes or until light and creamy. Add the egg and mix well. Stir in the chocolate chips.

Roll the dough into 20 g (¾ oz) balls and place on the trays 3 cm–5 cm (1¼ inches–2 inches) apart. Flatten each with the palm of your hand or the base of a floured glass. Bake for 7 minutes or until fragrant. Cool for 2 minutes on the trays, then remove to wire racks and cool completely. Use immediately or store in an airtight container for up to 4 days.

Line 2 baking trays with baking paper. Use a small ice-cream scoop or melon baller to scoop out 20 balls of ice-cream, place on the trays and refrigerate for 2–3 minutes or until slightly softened. Place the balls on half of the cookies, then sandwich with the remaining cookies. Place on the trays and freeze until firm.

Working with one sandwich at a time, carefully dip half a sandwich in the melted chocolate and place on the tray. Repeat with the remaining sandwiches. Place in the freezer until ready to serve.

Note: To make slightly larger ice-cream sandwiches, roll the mixture into 25 g (1 oz) balls and bake for 8–9 minutes; makes 15 sandwiches. Alternatively, roll the mixture into 30 g (1 oz) balls and bake for 10–11 minutes; makes 13 sandwiches.

Makes 20

Ice-cream cake pops

80 g (2¾ oz) unsalted butter, at
    room temperature

125 g (4½ oz/1 cup) icing
    (confectioners') sugar

2 tablespoons cocoa powder

2 tablespoons pouring (single) cream

30 mini waffle ice-cream cones

500 g (1 lb 2 oz) dark chocolate
    (65% cocoa solids), melted

200 g (7 oz) white chocolate, melted

sprinkles to decorate

chocolate cake

110 g (3¾ oz) self-raising
    (self-rising) flour

40 g (1½ oz/⅓ cup) cocoa powder

200 g (7 oz) caster (superfine) sugar

80 g (2¾ oz) unsalted butter, at
    room temperature

125 g (4½ oz) dark chocolate
    (65% cocoa solids), finely
    chopped

2 eggs, lightly beaten

1 teaspoon natural vanilla extract

To make the cake, preheat the oven to 180°C (350°F/Gas 4). Grease and line a 22 cm (8½ inch) round cake tin with baking paper. Sift the flour and cocoa together into a large bowl. Combine the sugar and 125 ml (4½ fl oz/ ½ cup) boiling water in the top of a double boiler over medium heat and stir until dissolved. Add the butter and chopped chocolate and stir until melted and smooth. Cool slightly. Combine the egg and vanilla extract, add to the flour mixture and mix well. Add the chocolate mixture and mix well. Pour into the tin and bake for 30–35 minutes or until a skewer inserted into the centre comes out clean. Remove from the tin and cool completely on a wire rack. Finely crumble the cake into a large bowl.

Place the butter, icing sugar and cocoa in the bowl of an electric mixer and beat for 1–2 minutes or until light and creamy. Add the cream and mix well. Add to the cake crumbs and, using your hands, mix well; the mixture should stick together when squeezed.

Line 2 baking trays with baking paper. Roll the mixture into 30 g (1 oz) balls. Press each onto an ice-cream cone and freeze for 15 minutes or until firm.

Carefully dip each pop in the melted dark chocolate, gently twirling off excess. Stand in styrofoam to dry. Using a teaspoon, drip some white chocolate over the dark chocolate and coat with the sprinkles. Serve immediately or store in an airtight container in the refrigerator for up to 3–4 days.

Makes 30

Persian rose macarons

80 g (2¾ oz/¾ cup) almond meal (ground almonds)

40 g (1½ oz) pistachio kernels

220 g (7¾ oz) icing (confectioners') sugar

110 g (3¾ oz) eggwhite

30 g (1 oz) caster (superfine) sugar

green food colouring, paste or powdered is preferable

Line 2 baking trays with paper. Process the almond meal, pistachios and icing sugar in a food processor until the pistachios are finely chopped, then sift twice.

Place the eggwhite in the bowl of an electric mixer and beat on medium speed until frothy, then increase the speed while gradually adding the caster sugar. Beat until stiff peaks form. Mix in enough colouring for desired effect. Fold one-third into the almond mixture and combine well. Gently fold through the remaining eggwhite mixture; it should be glossy and thick, not thin and runny.

Transfer to a piping bag fitted with a 5 mm (¼ inch) plain nozzle and pipe 3 cm (1¼ inch) circles about 3 cm (1¼ inches) apart onto the trays. Leave at room temperature for 1–6 hours (depending on the humidity) or until a crust forms; the macarons should no longer be sticky to the touch.

Preheat oven to 140°C (275°F/Gas 1). Bake the macarons for 15–18 minutes until they rise slightly. Immediately slide the macarons and paper off the trays onto wire racks to cool completely.

rose buttercream

100 g (3½ oz) caster (superfine) sugar

2 eggwhites

185 g (6½ oz) unsalted butter, cubed
   and at room temperature

3 tablespoons rosewater

pink food colouring, paste or powdered
   is preferable

To make the buttercream, place the sugar and eggwhite in
the top of a double boiler over medium heat and whisk
for 3–4 minutes or until warm and the sugar has dissolved.
Remove from the heat. Using electric beaters, beat the
mixture on medium–high speed for 6–7 minutes or until
glossy and stiff peaks form. Reduce the speed and add
the butter, one cube at a time, beating well after each
addition. Mix in the rosewater and enough colouring for
the desired effect.

Transfer to a piping bag fitted with a 1 cm (½ inch) plain
nozzle and pipe about 1 teaspoon onto half the macarons.
Sandwich with the remaining macarons.

Makes about 30

Peanut macarons
with
salted caramel

80 g (2¾ oz/¾ cup) almond meal
(ground almonds)

40 g (1½ oz) roasted peanuts

220 g (7¾ oz) icing (confectioners')
sugar

110 g (3¾ oz) eggwhite

30 g (1 oz) caster (superfine) sugar

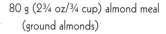

salted caramel filling

110 g (3¾ oz/½ cup) caster
(superfine) sugar

2 teaspoons glucose syrup

3 tablespoons pouring (single) cream

60 g (2¼ oz) butter, cubed and at
room temperature

¼ teaspoon fleur de sel or fine sea
salt flakes

Line 2 baking trays with baking paper. Process the almond meal, peanuts and icing sugar in a food processor until the peanuts are finely chopped, then sift twice. Place the eggwhite in the bowl of an electric mixer and beat on medium speed until frothy, then increase the speed while gradually adding the caster sugar. Beat until stiff peaks form. Fold one-third into the almond mixture and combine well. Gently fold through the remaining eggwhite mixture; it should be glossy and thick.

Transfer to a piping bag fitted with a 5 mm (¼ inch) nozzle and pipe 3 cm (1¼ inch) circles about 3 cm (1¼ inches) apart onto the trays. Leave for 1–6 hours or until a crust forms; the macarons should no longer be sticky.

Preheat the oven to 140°C (275°F/Gas 1). Bake the macarons for 15–18 minutes until they rise slightly. Immediately slide the macarons and paper off the trays onto wire racks to cool completely.

To make the filling, place the sugar, glucose and 1½ tablespoons water in a saucepan over medium–high heat, swirling the pan (do not stir) to dissolve the sugar. Increase the heat to high, bring to the boil and cook until golden. Remove from the heat and carefully add the cream. Place over low heat, add the butter, one cube at a time, beating well after each addition. Mix in the salt. Leave to cool until thickened.

Transfer to a piping bag fitted with a 1 cm (½ inch) nozzle and pipe about 1 teaspoon onto half of the macarons. Sandwich with the remaining macarons.

Makes about 30

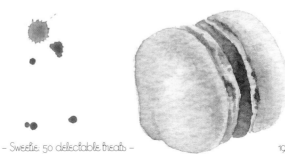

Layered jellies
with
citrus & pomegranate

4 small pomegranates, seeds removed

Persian fairy floss

blood orange jelly

500 ml (18 fl oz/2 cups) blood
 orange juice, strained

220 g (7¾ oz/1 cup) caster
 (superfine) sugar

1 tablespoon powdered gelatine

pomegranate jelly

500 ml (18 fl oz/2 cups) pomegranate
 juice, strained

165 g (5¾ oz/¾ cup) caster
 (superfine) sugar

1 tablespoon powdered gelatine

ruby grapefruit jelly

1 litre (35 fl oz/4 cups) ruby grapefruit
 juice, strained

220 g (7¾ oz/1 cup) caster
 (superfine) sugar

2 tablespoons powdered gelatine

To make the blood orange jelly, place the juice and sugar in a small saucepan over medium heat and stir until the sugar has dissolved. Remove from the heat, add the gelatine and stir until dissolved. Cool slightly, then divide among 16 x 125 ml (4½ fl oz/½ cup) capacity jelly moulds and refrigerate for 1 hour or until set.

To make the ruby grapefruit jelly, place the juice and sugar in a small saucepan over medium heat and stir until the sugar has dissolved. Remove from the heat, add the gelatine and stir until dissolved. Cool slightly, then distribute evenly into each of the moulds and refrigerate for 1 hour or until set.

To make the pomegranate jelly, place the juice and sugar into a small saucepan over medium heat and stir until the sugar has dissolved. Remove from the heat, add the gelatine and stir until dissolved. Cool slightly, then distribute evenly into each of the moulds and refrigerate for 1 hour or until set.

To serve, unmould the jellies onto serving plates, scatter around the pomegranate seeds and garnish with the fairy floss.

Makes 16

Meyer lemon bars

6 eggs

550 g (1 lb 4 oz/2½ cups) caster (superfine) sugar

75 g (2¾ oz/½ cup) plain (all-purpose) flour

250 ml (9 fl oz/1 cup) meyer lemon juice, strained (see note)

3 tablespoons finely grated meyer lemon zest

sweet crust

225 g (8 oz/1½ cups) plain (all-purpose) flour

65 g (2⅓ oz/½ cup) icing (confectioners') sugar, plus extra for dusting

180 g (6⅓ oz) unsalted butter, cut into 10 pieces

Preheat the oven to 180°C (350°F/Gas 4).

To make the crust, place the flour and sugar in the bowl of a food processor and pulse to combine. Add the butter, one piece at a time, until the mixture resembles pea-sized crumbs.

Press the mixture into the base of a 23.5 cm x 33.5 cm (9¼ inch x 13¼ inch) slice tin. Bake for 18–20 minutes or until golden. Cool in the tin for 20–30 minutes.

Reduce the temperature to 150°C (300°F/Gas 2). Whisk the eggs, sugar, flour and lemon juice together in a bowl until combined and smooth. Stir in the zest and pour over the crust. Bake for 25–30 minutes or until set. Remove from the oven and cool completely on a wire rack. Dust with the extra icing sugar and cut into 6 cm x 2.5 cm (2½ inch x 1 inch) bars.

Note: Meyer lemons are available in the cooler months from select greengrocers and farmers' markets

Makes 25

Glitter pops

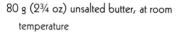

80 g (2¾ oz) unsalted butter, at room
temperature

250 g (9 oz/1 cup) cream cheese, at
room temperature

125 g (4½ oz/1 cup) icing
(confectioners') sugar

2 tablespoons white chocolate liqueur

50 lollipop sticks

650 g (1 lb 7 oz) white chocolate,
melted

75 g (2¾ oz/⅓ cup) gold sanding
sugar (see note)

white chocolate cake

300 g (10½ oz/2 cups) plain
(all-purpose) flour

2 teaspoons baking powder

¼ teaspoon salt

225 g (8 oz) unsalted butter, at room
temperature

440 g (15½ oz/2 cups) caster
(superfine) sugar

4 eggs

85 g (3 oz/⅓ cup) sour cream

65 ml (2¼ fl oz) white chocolate
liqueur

65 ml (2¼ fl oz) milk

1 tablespoon white vinegar

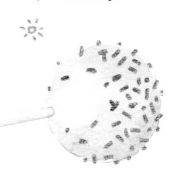

To make the cake, preheat the oven to 180°C (350°F/Gas 4). Grease and line a 31 cm x 21 cm x 5 cm (12½ inch x 8¼ inch x 2 inch) cake tin with baking paper. Sift the flour, baking powder and salt together into a bowl. Place the butter and sugar in the bowl of an electric mixer and beat on medium speed for 2–3 minutes or until light and creamy. Add the eggs, one at a time, beating well after each addition. Add the sour cream and liqueur and mix well. Add the milk and vinegar, in two batches, alternating with the flour mixture, scraping down the sides of the bowl as required. Pour into the tin and bake for 35–40 minutes or until a skewer inserted into the centre comes out clean. Cool completely in the tin. Slice off the sides, top and bottom of the cake and discard. Finely crumble the remaining cake into a large bowl.

Place the butter and cream cheese in the bowl of an electric mixer and beat on medium speed for 2 minutes or until smooth. Add the icing sugar and liqueur and mix well. Add to the cake crumbs and mix well; the mixture should stick together when squeezed in your hands.

Line 2 baking trays with baking paper and roll the mixture into 30 g (1 oz) balls. Insert a stick into each ball, place on the trays and refrigerate for 30 minutes or until chilled and firm.

Carefully dip each pop into the melted chocolate, gently twirling off any excess. Sprinkle with the sanding sugar and stand in styrofoam to dry. Serve immediately or store in an airtight container in the refrigerator for 3–4 days.

Note: Sanding sugar is available from specialist cake decorating shops or online.

Makes 45–50

Banana daiquiri cupcakes

150 g (5½ oz/1 cup) plain (all-purpose) flour

½ teaspoon bicarbonate of soda (baking soda)

¼ teaspoon baking powder

175 g (6 oz/about 2) mashed banana

3 tablespoons buttermilk

30 ml (1 fl oz) dark rum

65 g (2⅓ oz) unsalted butter, at room temperature

95 g (3⅓ oz/½ cup lightly packed) soft brown sugar

1 egg

coconut & rum frosting

2 eggwhites

110 g (3¾ oz/½ cup) caster (superfine) sugar

3 tablespoons glucose syrup

40 ml (1¼ fl oz) dark rum

1 teaspoon natural coconut extract

30 g (1 oz/½ cup) shredded coconut, toasted (optional)

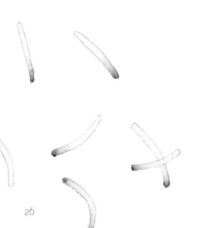

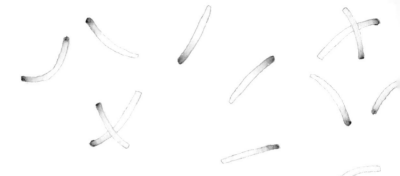

Preheat the oven to 180°C (350°F/Gas 4). Line 36 x 30 ml (1 fl oz/⅛ cup) capacity mini-muffin holes with paper cases.

Sift the flour, bicarbonate of soda and baking powder together into a bowl. Combine the banana, buttermilk and rum. Place the butter and sugar in the bowl of an electric mixer and beat on medium speed for 2–3 minutes or until light and creamy. Add the egg and beat well. Add the banana mixture, in three batches, alternating with the flour mixture, scraping down the sides of the bowl as required.

Transfer the batter to a large piping bag fitted with a 1 cm (½ inch) plain nozzle and pipe into the cases, filling them three-quarters full. Bake for 10 minutes or until lightly golden and they spring back lightly to the touch. Cool in the tins for 1–2 minutes, then turn out onto wire racks to cool completely.

To make the frosting, place the eggwhite, sugar, glucose and 2 tablespoons water in the top of a double boiler over medium heat and, using electric beaters, beat for 7–8 minutes or until glossy and stiff. Add the rum and coconut extract and beat for a further minute. Immediately frost the cupcakes and top with the shredded coconut.

Makes 36

Hazelnut macarons
with
chocolate & frangelico

60 g (2¼ oz) hazelnut meal (ground hazelnut), plus extra, for sprinkling

60 g (2¼ oz) almond meal (ground almond)

220 g (7¾ oz) icing (confectioners') sugar

110 g (3¾ oz) eggwhite

30 g (1 oz) caster (superfine) sugar

chocolate & frangelico ganache

110 g (3¾ oz) milk chocolate, chopped

3 tablespoons pouring (single) cream

50 ml (1¾ fl oz) frangelico

Line 2 baking trays with baking paper. Process the hazelnut and almond meal and icing sugar in a food processor until combined, then sift twice. Place the eggwhite in the bowl of an electric mixer and beat on medium speed until frothy, then increase the speed while gradually adding the caster sugar. Continue beating until stiff peaks form. Fold one-third into the hazelnut and almond mixture and combine well. Gently fold through the remaining eggwhite mixture; it should be glossy and thick, not thin and runny.

Transfer to a piping bag fitted with a 5 mm (¼ inch) plain nozzle and pipe 3 cm (1¼ inch) circles about 3 cm (1¼ inch) apart onto the trays. Leave at room temperature for 1–6 hours (depending on the humidity) or until a crust forms; the macarons should no longer be sticky to the touch.

Preheat the oven to 140°C (275°F/Gas 1). Bake the macarons for 15–18 minutes until they rise slightly. Immediately slide the macarons and paper off the trays onto wire racks to cool completely.

Meanwhile, to make the ganache, place all of the ingredients in the top of a double boiler over medium heat and stir until melted and smooth. Refrigerate for 20–25 minutes or until firm but pliable.

Transfer to a small piping bag fitted with a 1 cm (½ inch) plain nozzle and pipe about 1 teaspoon onto half of the macarons.

Sandwich with the remaining macarons.

Makes about 30

Persian Florentines

35 g (1¼ oz) chopped candied
    orange peel

100 g (3½ oz) dried sour cherries

80 g (2¾ oz) flaked almonds

65 g (2⅓ oz) pistachio kernels,
    chopped

1¼ teaspoon orange blossom water

35 g (1¼ oz/¼ cup) plain
    (all-purpose) flour

40 g (1½ oz) unsalted butter

60 g (2¼ oz) caster (superfine) sugar

60 g (2¼ oz) honey

80 ml (2½ fl oz/⅓ cup) pouring
    (single) cream

85 g (3 oz) dark chocolate
    (70% cocoa solids), melted

Preheat the oven to 175°C (340°F/Gas 3–4). Line 2 baking trays with baking paper.

Place the orange peel, cherries, nuts, orange blossom water and flour in a bowl and stir to combine.

Place the butter, sugar, honey and cream in a saucepan over medium heat, bring to the boil and cook until it reaches 112°C (234°F; soft-ball stage) on a candy thermometer. Add to the fruit and nut mixture and stir to combine.

Drop 1-tablespoon amounts of mixture about 5 cm (2 inches) apart on the trays and flatten slightly. Bake for 12–14 minutes or until golden and set. Cool on the trays completely.

Place the melted chocolate in a small piping bag fitted with a 5 mm (¼ inch) plain nozzle and pipe stripes across each cookie. Leave to set. Store in an airtight container for up to one week.

Makes 20

Pecan caramel tartlets

60 g (2¼ oz) unsalted butter

90 g (3¼ oz/¼ cup) dark corn syrup (see note)

1 tablespoon honey

65 g (2⅓ oz/½ cup) icing (confectioners') sugar

50 g (1¾ oz/½ cup) pecans, finely chopped

½ teaspoon natural vanilla extract

cream cheese pastry

125 g (4½ oz) butter, at room temperature

90 g (3¼ oz/⅓ cup) cream cheese, at room temperature

150 g (5½ oz/1 cup) plain (all-purpose) flour

30 g (1 oz/¼ cup) icing (confectioners') sugar

¼ teaspoon salt

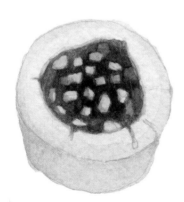
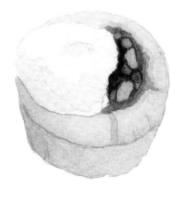

Preheat the oven to 180°C (350°F/Gas 4). Grease 24 x 30 ml (1 fl oz/⅛ cup) capacity mini-muffin holes.

To make the pastry, place the butter and cream cheese in the bowl of an electric mixer and beat on medium speed for 1–2 minutes or until combined. Add the flour, icing sugar and salt and beat to combine. Divide the pastry into 24 balls and place one in each muffin hole. Cover and refrigerate for 15–20 minutes.

Press the pastry into the base and sides of each hole. Cover and refrigerate until required.

Place the butter, corn syrup, honey and icing sugar in a saucepan over medium heat, bring to the boil and cook for 1 minute. Remove from the heat, add the pecans and vanilla extract and stir to combine. Spoon into the pastry cases and bake for 20–25 minutes or until set. Cool in the tins for 10 minutes, then remove and cool completely on wire racks.

Note: Dark corn syrup is available from speciality grocery shops.

Makes 24

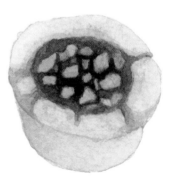

Warm apple pie bites

20 g (¾ oz) unsalted butter

400 g (14 oz/about 3) Granny Smith
apples, peeled, cored and diced

45 g (1⅔ oz/¼ cup lightly packed)
soft brown sugar

½ teaspoon ground cinnamon, plus
2 teaspoons ground cinnamon
extra, for coating

½ teaspoon ground nutmeg

2 tablespoons orange juice

2 teaspoons cornflour

2 teaspoons finely grated orange zest

220 g (7¾ oz/1 cup) caster
(superfine) sugar

vegetable oil for deep frying

dough

375 g (13 oz/2½ cups) plain
(all-purpose) flour

2 teaspoons caster (superfine) sugar

150 g (5½ oz) cold unsalted butter,
cut into 12 pieces

125 ml (4½ fl oz/½ cup) buttermilk

To make the dough, place the flour, sugar and butter in the bowl of a food processor and pulse until the mixture resembles breadcrumbs. Add the buttermilk and pulse until the dough comes together to form a ball. Turn out onto a floured surface, shape into a disc, wrap in plastic wrap and refrigerate for 2 hours.

Meanwhile, place the butter, apple, brown sugar, cinnamon and nutmeg into a frying pan over medium heat and cook for 5–6 minutes or until the apple has softened. Combine the orange juice and cornflour to make a paste, add to the apple mixture and cook for 1 minute or until thickened. Add the orange zest and cool to room temperature.

Roll out the dough on a floured surface to 3 mm (⅛ inch) and, using a 9 cm (3½ inch) round cutter, cut out circles. Re-roll the scraps and repeat. Place 2 teaspoons of apple mixture in the centre of each circle, fold in half and pinch the edges together firmly to seal. Refrigerate for 15–20 minutes.

Combine the caster sugar and extra cinnamon together in a shallow bowl and set aside.

Heat the oil in a deep-fryer or large, heavy-based frying pan to 175°C (340°F). Deep-fry the pies, 3–4 at a time, for 1–2 minutes on each side or until lightly golden. Drain on kitchen paper, then roll in the cinnamon sugar to coat. Serve immediately.

Makes 15–16

Almond corkscrews

60 g (2¼ oz) unsalted butter, at room
temperature

90 g (3¼ oz) caster (superfine) sugar

2 eggwhites, lightly beaten, at room
temperature

1 teaspoon natural almond extract

50 g (1¾ oz/⅓ cup) plain (all-
purpose) flour

65 g (2⅓ oz/¾ cup) toasted flaked
almonds

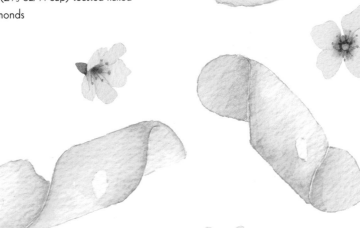

Preheat the oven to 180°C (350°F/Gas 4). Line 2 baking trays with baking paper.

Place the butter and sugar in the bowl of an electric mixer and beat on medium speed for 2–3 minutes or until light and fluffy. Gradually add the eggwhite and almond extract and beat well until combined. Add the flour and beat to combine.

Transfer to a large piping bag fitted with a 5 mm (¼ inch) plain nozzle. Pipe six 7 cm–8 cm (2¾ inch–3¼ inch) long lines about 5 cm (2 inches) apart onto one tray. Only prepare one tray of cookies to bake at a time. Scatter the lines with one-third of the almonds and bake for 4–5 minutes or until the edges begin to turn golden.

Remove from the oven. Working quickly, lift a cookie off the tray, using a spatula, then wrap it around the handle of a wooden spoon and leave to cool. Repeat with the remaining cookies. If the cookies cool and harden before being shaped, warm in the oven for 1 minute to soften. Slide the cooled corkscrews off the spoons. Repeat the process with the remaining mixture, piping lines onto a cool baking tray each time. Store the corkscrews in an airtight container for up to four days.

Makes 36

Glazed vanilla doughnuts
&
doughnut holes

250 g (9 oz/1⅔ cups) plain
  (all-purpose) flour

3 tablespoons caster (superfine) sugar

1 x 7 g (¼ oz) sachet dried yeast

½ teaspoon salt

80 ml (2½ fl oz/⅓ cup) milk

25 g (1 oz) unsalted butter

1 egg

vegetable oil, for deep-frying

glaze

125 g (4½ oz/1 cup) icing
  (confectioners') sugar

1½–2 teaspoons milk

½ teaspoon natural vanilla extract

sprinkles or 90 g (3¼ oz/¾ cup) icing
  (confectioners' sugar), for decoration

Line 2 baking trays with baking paper. Place 100 g (3½ oz) flour, sugar, yeast and salt in the bowl of an electric mixer and stir to combine. Place the milk and butter in a saucepan over medium heat and stir until melted. Add to the flour mixture and beat on medium speed to combine. Add the egg and beat for 2–3 minutes. Add the remaining flour and beat to combine well. Knead the dough on a floured surface for 3–4 minutes or until smooth. Place in a large oiled bowl, cover with plastic wrap and leave in a warm place for 1 hour or until doubled in size.

Roll out the dough on a floured surface to 5 mm (¼ inch) thick and, using a 5.5 cm (2¼ inch) round cutter, cut out circles. Use a 1 cm (½ inch) round cutter to cut out holes from the centre. Place the rings and holes on the trays. Re-roll the scraps and repeat. Cover and leave in a warm place for 35–40 minutes or until doubled in size.

Heat the oil in a deep-fryer or wide, heavy-based frying pan over medium heat to 175°C (340°F). Deep-fry the rings and holes, in batches, turning often, until golden. Drain on kitchen paper, then place on wire racks to cool completely.

To make the glaze, combine the icing sugar, milk and vanilla extract in a bowl. Spoon over the rings and holes.

To decorate, top with the sprinkles. Alternatively, for powdered doughnuts and holes, coat well in the sugar.

Makes about 30

Chocolate tarts with raspberry

400 g (14 oz) dark chocolate
  (65% cocoa solids), finely
  chopped

550 ml (19 fl oz) thickened cream

2 tablespoons natural raspberry extract
  (optional)

50 fresh raspberries

chocolate shortcrust pastry

175 g (6 oz) plain (all-purpose) flour

25 g (1 oz) cocoa powder

125 g (4½ oz) unsalted butter, at
  room temperature

80 g (2¾ oz) icing (confectioners')
  sugar

1 egg yolk

Place the chocolate and cream in the top of a double boiler over medium heat and stir until melted and smooth. Mix in the raspberry extract, if using. Transfer to a bowl and refrigerate for 20 minutes. Remove and stir, then refrigerate for a further 20 minutes. Repeat the process twice more and continue chilling for 4 hours or overnight.

Meanwhile, to make the pastry, sift the flour and cocoa together into a bowl. Place the butter and icing sugar in the bowl of an electric mixer and beat for 1–2 minutes or until light and creamy. Add the egg yolk and combine well. Add the flour mixture and beat until just combined. Shape into a disc, wrap in plastic wrap and refrigerate for 1–2 hours.

Preheat the oven to 180°C (350°F/Gas 4).

Roll the dough into 50 x 8 g (¼ oz) balls. Place each ball in a 3.5 cm (1¼ inch) fluted tartlet tin and press the pastry into the base and sides. Freeze for 10 minutes.

Place the pastry cases on baking trays and bake for 7–9 minutes or until golden and cooked. If the pastry puffs up, use a teaspoon to gently push it down. Cool in the tins for 8–10 minutes, then turn out onto wire racks to cool completely.

Transfer the chocolate mixture to the bowl of an electric mixer and beat on medium speed for 1–2 minutes or until soft peaks form. Transfer to a large piping bag fitted with a 5 mm (¼ inch) plain nozzle and pipe into the cases. Top with a raspberry.

Makes about 50

Ginger whoopie pies
with
spiced candied ginger cream

260 g (9¼ oz/1¾ cups) plain
(all-purpose) flour

1 teaspoon bicarbonate of soda
(baking soda)

pinch of salt

1 teaspoon ground ginger

110 g (3¾ oz/½ cup) caster
(superfine) sugar

95 g (3⅓ oz/½ cup lightly packed)
brown sugar

125 g (4½ oz) unsalted butter, at
room temperature

½ teaspoon natural vanilla extract

1 egg

250 ml (9 fl oz/1 cup) milk

spiced candied ginger cream

375 g (13 oz/1½ cups) cream cheese,
at room temperature

75 g (2¾ oz) unsalted butter, at
room temperature

2 teaspoons maple syrup

125 g (4½ oz/1 cup) icing
(confectioners') sugar

1 teaspoon ground cinnamon

1 teaspoon ground nutmeg

35 g (1¼ oz) candied ginger,
chopped

Preheat the oven to 175°C (340°F/Gas 3–4). Grease and flour 2 baking trays or 3 whoopie pie tins. Sift the flour, bicarbonate of soda, salt and ginger together into a large bowl. Place the sugars and butter in the bowl of an electric mixer and beat on medium speed for 1–2 minutes or until light and creamy. Add the vanilla extract and egg and beat for a further minute. Reduce the speed and add the flour mixture, in three batches, alternating with the milk and beat until combined, scraping down the sides of the bowl as required.

Place 1½-tablespoon amounts of batter about 5 cm (2 inches) apart on the trays and bake for 8–10 minutes or until cooked through. Cool for 5 minutes on the trays, then transfer to wire racks to cool completely.

Meanwhile, to make the ginger cream, place the cream cheese and butter in the bowl of an electric mixer and beat on medium speed for 2–3 minutes or until combined and smooth. Reduce the speed and add the maple syrup, icing sugar and spices and beat until combined. Fold in the candied ginger, cover with plastic wrap and refrigerate for 20 minutes or until firm.

Transfer to a piping bag fitted with a 1 cm (½ inch) plain nozzle and pipe 2 tablespoons of filling onto half of the cookies. Sandwich with the remaining cookies.

Makes 15

Lemon meringue cupcakes

185 g (6½ oz/1¼ cups) plain (all-purpose) flour

1½ teaspoons baking powder

125 g (4½ oz) unsalted butter at room temperature

145 g (5¼ oz/⅔ cup) caster (superfine) sugar

2 eggs

125 ml (4½ fl oz/½ cup) milk

½ teaspoon natural lemon extract

1 tablespoon finely grated lemon zest

60 g (2¼ oz/¼ cup) store-bought lemon curd

meringue

130 g (4¾ oz) caster (superfine) sugar

95 g (3⅓ oz) eggwhite

⅛ teaspoon salt

Preheat the oven to 175°C (340°F/Gas 3–4). Line 12 x 80 ml (2½ fl oz/ ⅓ cup) capacity muffin holes with paper cases. Sift the flour and baking powder together into a bowl. Place the butter and sugar in the bowl of an electric mixer and beat for 2–3 minutes or until light and creamy. Add the eggs, one at a time, beating well after each addition. Add the flour mixture, in three batches, alternating with the milk and beat until combined, scraping down the sides of the bowl as required. Add the lemon extract and zest and beat to combine. Divide between the cases and bake for 18–20 minutes or until lightly golden and when a skewer inserted into the centre comes out clean. Cool in the tin for 4–5 minutes, then turn out onto wire racks to cool completely.

Using a melon baller, remove a scoop of cake from each cupcake. Fill each hole with 1–1½ tablespoons of lemon curd.

To make the meringue, place all of the ingredients in the top of the double boiler over medium heat and whisk continuously for 3–4 minutes or until the mixture is hot to the touch and reaches 50°C (122°F) on a candy thermometer. Remove the bowl from the heat and, using electric beaters, beat the mixture on high speed until glossy and stiff peaks form. Immediately cover each cupcake with meringue, using a spatula, then lightly toast with a kitchen blowtorch.

Makes 12

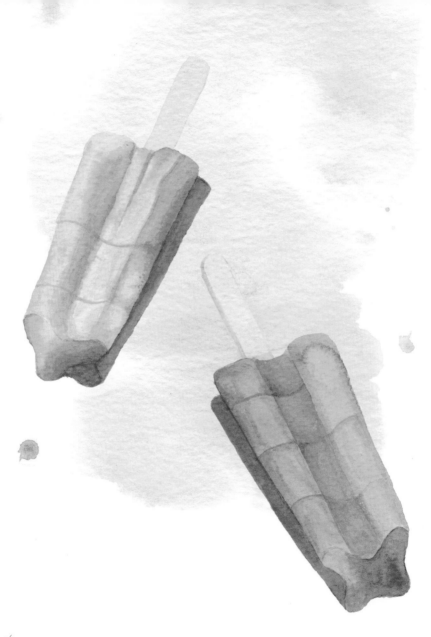

Hibiscus vodka pops

12 g (½ oz/¼ cup) dried hibiscus flowers
   or 3 hibiscus tea bags (see note)

60 ml (2 fl oz/¼ cup) agave syrup
   (see note)

60 ml (2 fl oz/¼ cup) vodka

10 popsicle sticks

Place the hibiscus flowers or tea bags in a heatproof jug, add 500 ml (18 fl oz/
2 cups) boiling water and leave for 15 minutes to infuse.

Remove the flowers or tea bags, add the agave syrup and stir until dissolved.
Add the vodka and leave to cool slightly.

Pour into 10 x 60 ml (2 fl oz/¼ cup) capacity popsicle moulds. Cover with plastic
wrap and insert a stick through the plastic into each pop. Freeze for 8–10 hours
or until completely frozen.

Note: Dried hibiscus flowers and agave syrup are available from health food shops.

Makes 10

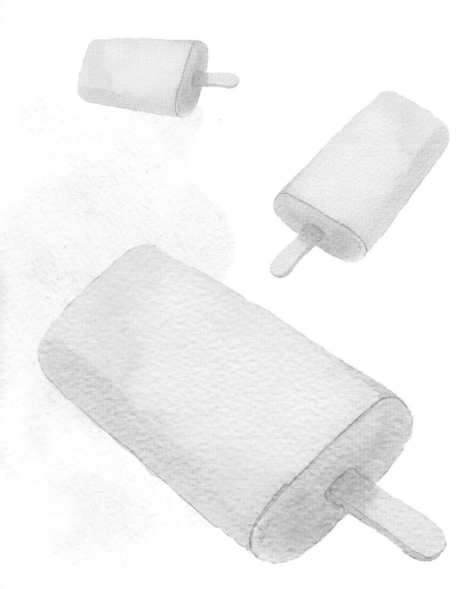

Mango lassi rum pops

550 ml (19 fl oz) mango pulp

120 ml (4 fl oz) white rum

120 ml (4 fl oz) orange juice

250 g (9 oz/1 cup) honey-flavoured
  yoghurt

4 tablespoons honey

½ teaspoon ground cardamom

1 teaspoon orange blossom water

18 popsicle sticks

Place all of the ingredients, except the sticks, in a large measuring jug and whisk to combine.

Pour into 18 x 60 ml (2 fl oz/¼ cup) capacity popsicle moulds. Cover with plastic wrap and insert a stick through the plastic into each pop. Freeze for 8–10 hours or until completely frozen.

Makes 18

Blueberry mojito popsicles

110 g (3¾ oz/½ cup) golden caster (superfine) sugar

¼ cup chopped mint

115 g (4 oz/¾ cup) fresh blueberries

3 tablespoons lime juice

75 ml (2⅓ fl oz rum)

300 ml (10½ fl oz) soda water

12 popsicle sticks

Place the sugar, mint, blueberries, lime juice and 3 tablespoons water in a saucepan over medium heat and simmer for 1–2 minutes or until the sugar has dissolved. Remove from the heat and leave to cool for 5 minutes to infuse.

Add the rum and soda water to the blueberry syrup and stir to combine. Pour into 12 x 60 ml (2 fl oz/¼ cup) capacity popsicle moulds. Cover with plastic wrap and insert a stick through the plastic into each pop. Freeze for 8–10 hours or until completely frozen.

Makes 12

Gingersnap & peach ice-cream sandwiches

gingersnap cookies

300 g (10½ oz/2 cups) plain
  (all-purpose) flour

1½ teaspoons bicarbonate of soda
  (baking soda)

2 teaspoons ground cinnamon

1 teaspoon ground allspice

½ teaspoon salt

125 g (4½ oz) unsalted butter,
  at room temperature

220 g (7¾ oz/1 cup) golden caster
  (superfine) sugar (see note)

1 egg, lightly beaten

85 ml (4 fl oz/¼ cup) unsulphured
  blackstrap molasses (see note)

2 teaspoons freshly grated ginger

½ cup minced candied ginger

140 g (5 oz/⅔ cup) raw (demerara)
  sugar

1.5 litres (52 fl oz/6 cups) peach
  ice-cream

52

To make the cookies, preheat the oven to 180°C (350°F/Gas 4). Line 2 baking trays with baking paper. Sift the flour, bicarbonate of soda, spices and salt together into a bowl. Place the butter and caster sugar in the bowl of an electric mixer and beat on medium speed for 2–3 minutes or until light and creamy. Add the egg and molasses and mix well. Add the flour mixture and gingers and mix well, scraping down the sides of the bowl.

Roll the dough into 15 g (½ oz) balls. Roll each in the raw sugar, place 3 cm–5 cm (1¼ inches–2 inches) apart on the trays and flatten with the base of a glass dipped in raw sugar. Bake for 7–9 minutes or until crisp. Cool completely on the trays. Use immediately or store in an airtight container for up to four days.

Line 2 baking trays with baking paper. Use a small ice-cream scoop or melon baller to scoop out 30 balls of ice-cream, place on the trays and refrigerate for 2–3 minutes or until slightly softened. Place the balls on half of the cookies and sandwich with the remaining cookies. Place in the freezer until ready to serve.

Note: Golden caster sugar is available from gourmet food shops. Blackstrap molasses is available from health food shops. To make slightly larger ice-cream sandwiches, roll the dough into 30 g (1 oz) balls and bake for 12–15 minutes; makes 15 sandwiches. Alternatively, roll the mixture into 20 g (¾ oz) balls and bake for 10–12 minutes; makes 20 sandwiches.

Makes 30

Black cherry
&
Kirsch jellies

1 litre (35 fl oz/4 cups) cherry juice

130 ml (4¼ fl oz) kirsch (cherry
   liqueur)

200 g (7 oz) caster (superfine) sugar

1½ tablespoons powdered gelatine

20 cherries, pitted and halved

dried miniature roses, for garnish

Place the cherry juice, kirsch and sugar in a saucepan over medium heat and bring to a simmer, stirring until the sugar has dissolved. Remove from the heat.

Add the gelatine and stir until dissolved. Cool to room temperature, then divide among 12 x 100 ml (3½ fl oz) capacity jelly moulds. Divide the cherries among the moulds and refrigerate for 2–3 hours or until set.

To serve, turn out and garnish with the roses.

Makes 12

Spiced pumpkin whoopie pies with pecan mascarpone

150 g (5½ oz/1 cup) plain
(all-purpose) flour

1 teaspoon ground cinnamon

½ teaspoon ground nutmeg

¼ teaspoon ground cloves

½ teaspoon bicarbonate of soda
(baking soda)

½ teaspoon baking powder

185 g (6½ oz/1 cup lightly packed)
soft brown sugar

125 g (4½ oz) unsalted butter, at
room temperature

1 egg

250 g (9 oz/1 cup) pumpkin purée
(see note)

½ teaspoon natural vanilla extract

125 ml (4½ fl oz/½ cup) milk

pecan mascarpone

250 ml (9 fl oz/1 cup) pouring
(single) cream

300 g (10½ oz) mascarpone, at room
temperature

1 teaspoon natural vanilla extract

125 g (4½ oz/1 cup) icing
(confectioners') sugar, sifted

½ teaspoon ground nutmeg

35 g (1¼ oz/ ⅓ cup) roasted pecans,
chopped

Preheat the oven to 175°C (340°F/Gas 3–4). Grease and flour 2 baking trays or 3 whoopie pie tins. Sift the flour, spices, bicarbonate of soda and baking powder together into a large bowl. Place the sugar and butter in the bowl of an electric mixer and beat on medium speed for 1–2 minutes or until light and creamy. Add the egg, pumpkin and vanilla extract and beat to combine well. Reduce the speed and add the flour mixture, in three batches, alternating with the milk and beat until combined, scraping down the sides of the bowl as required.

Place 1½-tablespoon amounts of batter about 5 cm (2 inches) apart on the trays and bake for 9–12 minutes or until cooked through. Cool for 5 minutes on the trays, then transfer to wire racks to cool completely.

To make the pecan mascarpone, whisk the cream until soft peaks form. Place the mascarpone and vanilla extract in the bowl of an electric mixer and beat on medium speed for 1–2 minutes or until combined and smooth. Reduce the speed, add the icing sugar and nutmeg and beat until combined. Fold in the whipped cream and the pecans. Cover with plastic wrap and refrigerate for 20 minutes or until firm.

Transfer to a piping bag fitted with a 1 cm (½ inch) plain nozzle and pipe 2 tablespoons of filling onto half of the cookies. Sandwich with the remaining cookies.

Note: To make pumpkin purée, roast the pumpkin in a preheated 200°C (400°F/Gas 6) oven until tender, then process in a food processor until it becomes a smooth purée. Cool.

Makes 16

Strawberry tartlets
with
sticky balsamic glaze

300 g (10½ oz) goat's curd

200 g (7 oz) ricotta

3 teaspoons orange blossom honey

1 teaspoon finely grated orange zest

25 strawberries, halved

vanilla shortcrust pastry

125 g (4½ oz) unsalted butter, at
room temperature

80 g (2¾ oz) icing (confectioners')
sugar

1 egg yolk

½ vanilla bean, split and seeds
scraped

200 g (7 oz/1⅓ cups) plain (all-
purpose) flour, sifted

balsamic glaze

125 ml (4½ fl oz/½ cup) good-quality
balsamic vinegar

115 g (4 oz/⅓ cup) honey

To make the pastry, place the butter and icing sugar in the bowl of an electric mixer and beat for 2–3 minutes or until light and creamy. Add the egg yolk and vanilla seeds and beat to combine well. Add the flour and beat until just combined. Turn the dough out onto a floured surface, shape into a disc, wrap in plastic wrap and refrigerate for 1–2 hours.

Preheat the oven to 180°C (350°F/Gas 4).

Meanwhile, to make the glaze, place the vinegar and honey in a saucepan over medium heat and simmer until reduced by one-third and the mixture is thick and syrupy. Cool completely.

Roll the dough into 50 x 8 g (¼ oz) balls. Place each ball into a 3.5 cm (1¼ inch) fluted tartlet tin and press the pastry into the base and sides. Freeze for 10 minutes.

Place the pastry cases on baking trays and bake for 7–9 minutes or until golden and cooked. If the pastry puffs up, use a teaspoon to gently push it down. Cool in the tins for 8–10 minutes, then turn out onto wire racks and cool completely.

To serve, combine the goat's curd, ricotta, honey and orange zest in a bowl. Transfer to a large piping bag fitted with a 5 mm (¼ inch) plain nozzle and pipe the mixture into the cases. Top each with a strawberry half and drizzle with the balsamic glaze.

Makes about 50

Passionfruit macarons

120 g (4¼ oz) almond meal (ground almonds)

220 g (7¾ oz) icing (confectioners') sugar

110 g (3¾ oz) eggwhite

30 g (1 oz) caster (superfine) sugar

yellow food colouring, paste or powdered is preferable

passionfruit curd

5 egg yolks

165 g (5¾ oz/¾ cup) caster (superfine) sugar

125 ml (4½ fl oz/½ cup) passionfruit pulp

1 tablespoon lemon juice

80 g (2¾ oz) unsalted butter, cubed

Line 2 baking trays with baking paper. Process the almond meal and icing sugar in a food processor until combined, then sift twice. Place the eggwhite in the bowl of an electric mixer and beat on medium speed until frothy, then increase the speed while gradually adding the caster sugar. Continue beating until stiff peaks form. Mix in enough colouring for desired effect. Fold one-third into the almond mixture and combine well. Gently fold through the remaining eggwhite mixture; it should be glossy and thick, not thin and runny.

Transfer to a piping bag fitted with a 5 mm (¼ inch) plain nozzle and pipe 3 cm (1¼ inch) circles about 3 cm (1¼ inches) apart onto the trays. Leave for 1–6 hours (depending on the humidity) or until a crust forms; the macarons should no longer be sticky.

To make the curd, place the egg yolks, sugar, pulp and lemon juice in a saucepan over medium–low heat and, using a wooden spoon, stir continuously for 8–9 minutes or until thick and the mixture coats the spoon. Remove from the heat and add the butter, one cube at a time, beating well after each addition. Cover with plastic wrap and refrigerate for 1 hour.

Preheat the oven to 140°C (275°F/Gas 1). Bake the macarons for 15–18 minutes until they rise slightly. Immediately slide the macarons and paper off the trays onto wire racks to cool completely.

Transfer the curd to a piping bag fitted with a 1 cm (½ inch) plain nozzle and pipe about 1 teaspoon onto half of the macarons. Sandwich with the remaining macarons.

Makes about 30

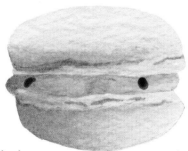

Pimm's pops

250 ml (9 fl oz/1 cup) ginger ale

250 ml (9 fl oz/1 cup) lemonade

185 ml (6 fl oz/¾ cup) Pimm's

8 mint leaves

2 orange slices

2 lemon slices

4 small cucumber slices

4 strawberries, halved

10 popsicle sticks

Place all the ingredients, except the sticks, in a large measuring jug and refrigerate for 1–2 hours to infuse.

Pour the Pimm's mixture into 10 x 60 ml (2 fl oz/¼ cup) capacity popsicle moulds and add a mint leaf, piece of fruit or slice of cucumber to each popsicle. Cover with plastic wrap and insert a stick through the plastic into each pop. Freeze for 8–10 hours or until completely frozen.

Makes 10

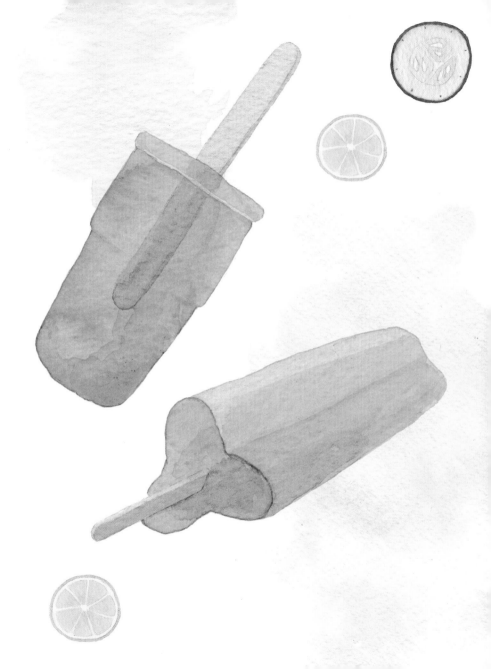

G & T pops

85 ml (2¾ fl oz) lemon juice

60 ml (2 fl oz/¼ cup) lime juice

165 g (5¾ oz/¾ cup) caster
(superfine) sugar

10 small lime or lemon slices

300 ml (10½ fl oz) tonic water

65 ml (2¼ fl oz) gin

10 popsicle sticks

Place the lemon and lime juices, sugar and lime slices in a non-reactive saucepan over medium heat and simmer for 1–2 minutes or until the sugar has dissolved. Remove from the heat and leave to cool for 5 minutes.

Add the tonic water and gin to the lemon syrup and stir to combine. Pour into 10 x 60 ml (2 fl oz/¼ cup) popsicle moulds and add a lime slice to each. Cover with plastic wrap and insert stick through the plastic into each pop. Freeze for 8–10 hours or until completely frozen.

Makes 10

Tangerine mimosa jellies

400 ml (14 fl oz) tangerine juice, strained

1.1 litres (38½ fl oz) sparkling white wine

400 g (14 oz) caster (superfine) sugar

2 tablespoons powdered gelatine

Persian fairy floss, to garnish

Place the juice, wine and sugar in a saucepan over medium–low heat and bring to a simmer, stirring until the sugar has dissolved. Remove from the heat.

Add the gelatine and stir until dissolved. Cool to room temperature, then pour into 12 champagne glasses and refrigerate for 2–3 hours or until set.

To serve, garnish with the fairy floss.

Makes 12

Jelly appletinis

1 litre (35 fl oz/4 cups) apple juice

120 ml (4 fl oz) vodka

15 ml (½ fl oz) apple schnapps

200 g (7 oz) caster (superfine) sugar

1½ tablespoons powdered gelatine

apple slices, for garnish

Place the juice, vodka, schnapps and sugar in a saucepan over medium heat and bring to a simmer, stirring until the sugar has dissolved. Remove from the heat.

Add the gelatine and stir until dissolved. Cool to room temperature, then divide among 12 x 100 ml (3½ fl oz) capacity jelly moulds. Refrigerate for 2–3 hours or until set.

Garnish with apple slices to serve.

Makes 12

Mini coconut cakes

125 g (4½ oz) butter, at room
   temperature
165 g (5¾ oz/¾ cup) caster
   (superfine) sugar
1 egg
2 egg yolks
2 teaspoons natural coconut extract
125 ml (4½ fl oz/½ cup) coconut milk
185 g (6½ oz/1¼ cup) plain (all-
   purpose) flour
¼ teaspoon baking powder
¼ teaspoon bicarbonate of soda
   (baking soda)
35 g (1¼ oz/⅔ cup) coconut flakes

coconut frosting

2 eggwhites
110 g (3¾ oz/½ cup) caster
   (superfine) sugar
3 tablespoons glucose syrup
icing flowers or 30 g (1 oz/½ cup)
   coconut flakes, toasted, for garnish

Preheat the oven to 180°C (350°F/Gas 4). Grease and flour a 12 x 125 ml (4½ oz/½ cup) capacity friand tin.

Place the butter and sugar in the bowl of an electric mixer and beat on medium speed for 1–2 minutes or until light and creamy. Add the egg and egg yolks, one at a time, beating well after each addition. Mix in the coconut extract and coconut milk. Add the flour, baking powder and bicarbonate of soda and beat for 1 minute. Mix in the coconut flakes.

Divide the mixture between the friand moulds and bake for 20–25 minutes or until golden and the cakes spring back lightly to the touch. Cool in the tin for 10 minutes, then turn out onto wire racks to cool completely.

To make the frosting, place the eggwhites, sugar, glucose and 2 tablespoons water in the top of a double boiler over medium heat and, using an electric beater, beat for 7 minutes or until stiff peaks form. Immediately frost the cakes and garnish with icing flowers or coconut flakes.

Makes 12

Blood orange macarons

120 g (4¼ oz) almond meal (ground almonds)

220 g (7¾ oz) icing (confectioners') sugar

110 g (3¾ oz) eggwhite

30 g (1 oz) caster (superfine) sugar

1 teaspoon natural orange extract

orange or red food colouring, paste or powdered is preferable

blood orange curd

6 egg yolks

125 ml (4½ fl oz/½ cup) blood orange juice, strained

1½ tablespoons lemon juice

165 g (5¾ oz/¾ cup) caster (superfine) sugar

80 g (2¾ oz) unsalted butter, cubed

Line 2 baking trays with baking paper. Process the almond meal and icing sugar in a food processor until combined, then sift twice. Place the eggwhite in the bowl of an electric mixer and beat on medium speed until frothy, then increase the speed while gradually adding the caster sugar. Continue beating until soft peaks form. Mix in the orange extract and colouring. Fold one-third into the almond mixture and combine well. Gently fold through the remaining eggwhite mixture; it should be glossy and thick, not thin and runny.

Transfer to a piping bag fitted with a 5 mm (¼ inch) plain nozzle and pipe 3 cm (1¼ inch) circles about 3 cm (1¼ inches) apart onto the trays. Leave for 1—6 hours (depending on the humidity) or until a crust forms; the macarons should no longer be sticky.

To make the curd, place the egg yolks, juices and sugar in a saucepan over medium—low heat and stir continuously for 8—9 minutes or until thick and the mixture coats a wooden spoon. Remove from the heat and add the butter, one cube at a time, beating well after each addition. Cover with plastic wrap and refrigerate for 1 hour.

Preheat the oven to 140°C (275°F/Gas 1). Bake the macarons for 15—18 minutes until they rise slightly. Immediately slide the macarons and paper off the trays onto wire racks to cool completely.

Transfer the curd to a piping bag fitted with a 1 cm (½ inch) plain nozzle and pipe about 1 teaspoon onto half of the macarons. Sandwich with the remaining macarons.

Makes about 30

Rocky road pops

80 g (2¾ oz) unsalted butter, at room
temperature

125 g (4½ oz/1 cup) icing
(confectioners') sugar

2 tablespoons cocoa powder

2 tablespoons pouring (single) cream

60 mini marshmallows

30 lollipop sticks

500 g (1 lb 2 oz) dark chocolate
(65% cocoa solids), melted

125 g (4½ oz/1 cup) finely chopped
walnuts

chocolate cake

110 g (3¾ oz/¾ cup) self-raising
(self-rising) flour

40 g (1½ oz/⅓ cup) cocoa powder

200 g (7 oz) caster (superfine) sugar

80 g (2¾ oz) unsalted butter, at room
temperature

125 g (4½ oz) dark chocolate
(65% cocoa solids), finely chopped

2 eggs, lightly beaten

1 teaspoon natural vanilla extract

To make the cake, preheat the oven to 180°C (350°F/Gas 4). Grease and line a 22 cm (8½ inch) round cake tin with baking paper. Sift the flour and cocoa together into a large bowl. Combine the sugar and 125 ml (4½ fl oz/ ½ cup) boiling water in the top of a double boiler over medium heat and stir until dissolved. Add the butter and chocolate and stir until melted and smooth. Cool slightly. Combine the egg and vanilla extract, add to the flour mixture and mix well. Add the chocolate mixture and mix well. Pour into the tin and bake for 30–35 minutes or until a skewer inserted into the centre comes out clean. Remove from the tin and cool completely on a wire rack. Finely crumble the cake into a large bowl.

Place the butter, icing sugar and cocoa in the bowl of an electric mixer and beat for 1–2 minutes or until light and creamy. Add the cream and mix well. Add to the cake crumbs and, using your hands, mix well; the mixture should stick together when squeezed.

Line 2 baking trays with baking paper. Roll the mixture into 30 g (1 oz) balls. Push 2 marshmallows into the centre of each and roll to enclose. Insert a stick into each, place on the trays and refrigerate for 30 minutes or until chilled and firm.

Carefully dip each pop in the chocolate, gently twirling off excess. Roll each in the walnuts to coat well. Stand in styrofoam to dry. Serve immediately or store in an airtight container in the refrigerator for up to 3–4 days.

Makes 30

Watermelon margarita pops with sweet & salty lime wedges

550 g (1 lb 4 oz) seedless
   watermelon, rind removed and cut
   into small chunks

40 ml (1¼ fl oz) lime juice

40 ml (1¼ fl oz) agave syrup
   (see note)

45 ml (1⅔ fl oz) tequila

15 ml (½ fl oz) Cointreau

12 popsicle sticks

2 tablespoons fine sea salt

2 tablespoons caster (superfine) sugar

10 lime wedges

10 skewers

Combine the watermelon, lime juice, agave syrup, tequila and Cointreau in a bowl and leave for 20 minutes. Transfer to a blender and pulse until juicy but with chunks of watermelon remaining.

Pour into 12 x 60 ml (2 fl oz/¼ cup) popsicle moulds. Cover with plastic wrap and insert a stick through the plastic into each pop. Freeze for 8–10 hours or until completely frozen.

To serve, place the salt and sugar on separate plates. Dip one side of each lime wedge in the salt, then the other side in the sugar. Skewer a lime wedge through the bottom of each stick.

Note: Agave syrup is available from health food shops.

Makes 12

Lemon madeleines
with
limoncello glaze

130 g (4¾ oz) plain (all-purpose)
  flour

½ teaspoon baking powder

3 eggs

130 g (4¾ oz) caster (superfine) sugar

2 tablespoons finely grated lemon zest

1 teaspoon natural lemon extract

115 g (4 oz) unsalted butter, melted

limoncello glaze

190 g (6¾ oz/1½ cups) icing
  (confectioners') sugar

2 tablespoons lemon juice

40 ml (1¼ fl oz) limoncello

Preheat the oven to 180°C (350°F/Gas 4). Grease 2 madeleine tins.

Sift the flour and baking powder together into a bowl. Place the eggs, sugar and lemon zest and extract in the bowl of an electric mixer and whisk on medium–high speed for 4–5 minutes or until pale and thickened. Gently fold in the flour mixture. Fold in the butter, a little at a time, folding well after each addition. Leave to rest for 15–20 minutes.

Meanwhile, to make the glaze, whisk all of the ingredients in a bowl until combined and smooth. Set aside.

Fill the tins with the madeleine mixture until three-quarters full and bake for 7–9 minutes or until the edges are light golden. Turn out onto wire racks and cool for 2–3 minutes, then spoon over the glaze to coat.

Repeat with the remaining batter. Madeleines are best eaten on the day of making.

Makes 48

Churros
with
chilli-chocolate sauce

vegetable oil, for deep-frying

125 g (4½ oz) unsalted butter

¼ teaspoon salt

150 g (5½ oz/1 cup) plain
(all-purpose) flour

2 eggs

145 g (5¼ oz/⅔ cup) caster
(superfine) sugar

1½ teaspoons ground cinnamon

chocolate-chilli sauce

150 ml (5 fl oz) pouring (single) cream

150 g (5½ oz) dark chocolate chips
(65% cocoa solids)

1 teaspoon natural vanilla extract

½ teaspoon ancho chilli powder
(see note)

½ teaspoon ground cinnamon

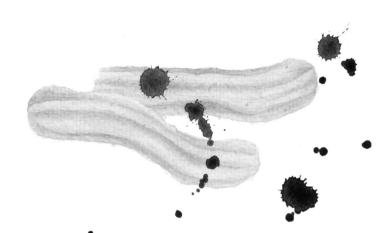

Heat the oil in a deep-fryer or wide, heavy-based frying pan to 175°C (340°F/ Gas 4).

Place the butter, salt and 250 ml (9 fl oz/1 cup) water in a saucepan over medium heat and bring to the boil. Add the flour and stir vigorously with a wooden spoon until the dough comes together to form a ball. Remove from the heat and add the eggs, beating well to combine; the dough should be shiny and soft.

Transfer to a large piping bag fitted with a small star nozzle. Carefully hold the piping bag over the oil with one hand and a small knife in the other. Place the dough into the oil and use the knife to slice off 7 cm (2¾ inch) lengths. Deep-fry 10–12 churros at a time for 2–3 minutes or until golden and crisp. Drain on kitchen paper and keep warm. Repeat with the remaining dough.

Combine the sugar and cinnamon in a shallow bowl and roll the churros in the mixture to coat.

To make the sauce, place the cream and chocolate in the top of a double boiler over medium heat and stir until melted and smooth. Add the vanilla extract, chilli powder and cinnamon and stir to combine. Remove from the heat and keep warm.

Serve the churros with the sauce for dipping.

Note: Ancho chilli powder is available from gourmet food shops and delicatessens.

Makes about 70

Vanilla whoopie pies
with
white chocolate chips

260 g (9¼ oz/1¾ cups) plain
   (all-purpose) flour

1 teaspoon bicarbonate of soda
   (baking soda)

pinch of salt

110 g (3¾ oz/½ cup) caster
   (superfine) sugar

95 g (3⅓ oz/½ cup lightly packed)
   soft brown sugar

125 g (4½ oz) unsalted butter

1 vanilla bean, split and seeds scraped

1 egg

250 ml (9 fl oz/1 cup) milk

170 g (6 oz/1 cup) mini white
   chocolate chips, for decoration

vanilla buttercream

3 eggwhites

145 g (5¼ oz/⅔ cup) caster
   (superfine) sugar

160 g (5⅔ oz) unsalted butter, cubed
   and at room temperature

1 vanilla bean, split and seeds scraped

Preheat the oven to 175°C (340°F/Gas 3–4). Grease and flour 2 baking trays or 3 whoopie pie tins. Sift the flour, bicarbonate of soda and salt together into a large bowl. Place the caster sugar, soft brown sugar and butter in the bowl of an electric mixer and beat on medium speed for 1–2 minutes or until light and creamy. Add the vanilla seeds and egg and beat for a further minute. Reduce the speed and add the flour mixture, in three batches, alternating with the milk and beat until combined, scraping down the sides of the bowl as required.

Place 1½-tablespoon amounts of batter about 5 cm (2 inches) apart on the trays and bake for 8–10 minutes or until cooked through. Cool for 5 minutes on the trays, then transfer to wire racks to cool completely.

Meanwhile, to make the buttercream, place the eggwhites and sugar in the top of a double boiler over medium heat and whisk for 3–4 minutes or until warm and the sugar has dissolved. Remove from the heat. Using electric beaters, beat the mixture on medium–high speed for 6–7 minutes or until glossy and stiff peaks form. Reduce the speed and add the butter, one cube at a time, beating well after each addition. Continue to beat for 2–3 minutes. Add the vanilla seeds and beat to combine.

Transfer to a piping bag fitted with a 1 cm (½ inch) plain nozzle and pipe 2 tablespoons of filling onto half of the cookies. Sandwich with the remaining cookies and roll the sides of the pies in the chocolate chips to coat.

Makes 15

Black velvet whoopie pies

225 g (8 oz/1½ cups) plain
    (all-purpose) flour

60 g (2¼ oz/½ cup) cocoa powder

1 teaspoon bicarbonate of soda
    (baking soda)

pinch of salt

160 g (5⅔ oz/1 cup) brown sugar

125 g (4½ oz) unsalted butter, at
    room temperature

1 teaspoon natural vanilla extract

1 egg

250 ml (9 fl oz/1 cup) buttermilk

½ teaspoon white vinegar

cream cheese frosting

375 g (13 oz/1½ cups) cream cheese,
    at room temperature

75 g (2¾ oz) unsalted butter, at room
    temperature

1 teaspoon natural vanilla extract

125 g (4½ oz/1 cup) icing
    (confectioners') sugar, sifted

Preheat the oven to 175°C (340°F/Gas 3–4). Grease and flour 2 baking trays or 3 whoopie pie tins. Sift the flour, cocoa, bicarbonate of soda and salt together into a large bowl. Place the sugar and butter in the bowl of an electric mixer and beat on medium speed for 1–2 minutes or until light and creamy. Add the vanilla extract and egg and beat for a further minute. Reduce the speed and add the flour mixture, in three batches, alternating with the buttermilk and beat until just combined, then beat in the vinegar, scraping down the sides of the bowl as required.

Place 1½-tablespoon amounts of batter about 5 cm (2 inches) apart on the trays and bake for 8–10 minutes or until cooked through. Cool for 5 minutes on the trays, then transfer to wire racks to cool completely.

Meanwhile, to make the frosting, place the cream cheese, butter and vanilla extract in the bowl of an electric mixer and beat on medium–high speed for 2–3 minutes or until combined and smooth. Reduce the speed, add the icing sugar and beat until combined. Cover with plastic wrap and refrigerate for 20–25 minutes or until firm.

Transfer to a piping bag fitted with a 1 cm (½ inch) plain nozzle and pipe 2 tablespoons of filling onto half of the cookies. Sandwich with the remaining cookies.

Makes 15

S'mores cupcakes

180 g (6⅓ oz) plain (all-purpose) flour

1 teaspoon baking powder

30 g (1 oz/¼ cup) cocoa powder

150 g (5½ oz) unsalted butter

150 g (5½ oz) caster (superfine) sugar

1 teaspoon natural vanilla extract

3 eggs

3 tablespoons milk

50 g (1¾ oz/⅓ cup) mini milk chocolate chips

cookie crumbs

2 wheat digestive biscuits, finely crushed

¾ teaspoon caster (superfine) sugar

¼ teaspoon ground cinnamon

chocolate sauce

85 g (3 oz/½ cup) mini milk chocolate chips

3 tablespoons pouring (single) cream

1 teaspoon unsalted butter

marshmallow frosting

3 eggwhites

165 g (5¾ oz/¾ cup) caster (superfine) sugar

¼ teaspoon cream of tartar

½ teaspoon natural vanilla extract

Preheat the oven to 180°C (350°F/Gas 4). Line 42 x 30 ml (1 fl oz/⅛ cup) capacity mini muffin holes with paper cases.

Sift the flour, baking powder and cocoa together into a bowl.

Place the butter, sugar and vanilla extract in the bowl of an electric mixer and beat on medium speed for 2–3 minutes or until light and creamy. Add the eggs, one at a time, beating well after each addition and scraping down the sides of the bowl as required. Add the flour mixture, in two batches, alternating with the milk. Add the chocolate chips and mix until just combined.

Transfer the batter to a large piping bag fitted with a 3 cm (1¼ inch) plain nozzle and pipe into the cases until three-quarters full.

Bake for 10–11 minutes or until just cooked and they spring back lightly to the touch. Cool for 1–2 minutes in the tins, then turn out onto wire racks to cool completely.

To make the cookie crumbs, place all of the ingredients in a bowl and combine well. Set aside.

To make the sauce, place the chocolate, cream and butter in the top of a double boiler over medium heat and stir until melted and smooth. Leave to cool slightly.

To make the frosting, place the eggwhites, sugar and cream of tartar in the top of a double boiler over medium heat and whisk for 3 minutes or until the sugar has dissolved and the mixture is warm. Remove from the heat, add the vanilla extract and, using electric beaters, beat for 6–7 minutes or until stiff peaks form. Immediately transfer into a piping bag fitted with a 1 cm (½ inch) plain nozzle and pipe onto the cupcakes. Lightly toast the frosting with a kitchen blowtorch, then drizzle each cupcake with the sauce and sprinkle with the crumbs.

Makes 42

Chocolate macarons
with
espresso & cocoa nibs

110 g (3¾ oz) almond meal (ground almonds)

15 g (½ oz) cocoa powder

200 g (7 oz) icing (confectioners') sugar

110 g (3¾ oz) eggwhite

30 g (1 oz) caster (superfine) sugar

espresso ganache

80 ml (2½ fl oz/⅓ cup) pouring (single) cream

2 teaspoons instant coffee granules

120 g (4¼ oz) dark chocolate (70% cocoa solids), chopped

2 tablespoons cocoa nibs (see note)

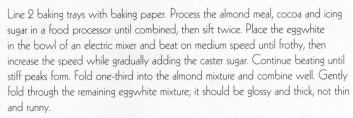

Line 2 baking trays with baking paper. Process the almond meal, cocoa and icing sugar in a food processor until combined, then sift twice. Place the eggwhite in the bowl of an electric mixer and beat on medium speed until frothy, then increase the speed while gradually adding the caster sugar. Continue beating until stiff peaks form. Fold one-third into the almond mixture and combine well. Gently fold through the remaining eggwhite mixture; it should be glossy and thick, not thin and runny.

Transfer to a piping bag fitted with a 5 mm (¼ inch) plain nozzle and pipe 3 cm (1¼ inch) circles about 3 cm (1¼ inches) apart onto the trays. Leave at room temperature for 1–6 hours (depending on the humidity) or until a crust forms; the macarons should no longer be sticky to the touch.

Preheat the oven to 140°C (275°F/Gas 1). Bake the macarons for 15–18 minutes until they rise slightly. Immediately slide the macarons and paper off the trays onto wire racks to cool completely.

Meanwhile, to make the ganache, place the cream and coffee granules in the top of a double boiler over medium heat and stir until the coffee has dissolved. Add the chocolate and stir until melted and smooth. Refrigerate for 20–25 minutes or until firm but pliable, then gently stir through the cocoa nibs.

Transfer to a small piping bag fitted with a 1 cm (½ inch) plain nozzle and pipe about 1 teaspoon onto half of the macarons. Sandwich with the remaining macarons.

Note: Cocoa nibs are available from gourmet food shops.

Makes about 30

Choc-mint whoopie pies
with
marshmallow frosting

150 g (5½ oz/1 cup) plain
    (all-purpose) flour

60 g (2¼ oz/½ cup) cocoa powder

½ teaspoon bicarbonate of soda
    (baking soda)

145 g (5¼ oz/⅔ cup) caster
    (superfine) sugar

90 g (3¼ oz) unsalted butter, at room
    temperature

½ teaspoon natural vanilla extract

1 teaspoon mint extract

1 egg

250 ml (9 fl oz/1 cup) milk

120 g (4¼ oz) crushed peppermint
    candies, for decoration

marshmallow frosting

3 eggwhites

165 g (5¾ oz/¾ cup) caster
    (superfine) sugar

¼ teaspoon cream of tartar

2 teaspoons peppermint schnapps

Preheat the oven to 175°C (340°F/Gas 3–4). Grease and flour 2 baking trays or 3 whoopie pie tins. Sift the flour, cocoa and bicarbonate of soda together into a large bowl. Place the sugar and butter in the bowl of an electric mixer and beat on medium speed for 1–2 minutes or until light and creamy. Add the vanilla and mint extracts and egg and beat for a further minute. Reduce the speed and add the flour mixture, in three batches, alternating with the milk and beat until combined, scraping down the sides of the bowl as required.

Place 1½-tablespoon amounts of batter about 5 cm (2 inches) apart on the trays and bake for 8–10 minutes or until cooked through. Cool for 5 minutes on the trays, then transfer to wire racks to cool completely.

Meanwhile, to make the frosting, place the eggwhites, sugar and cream of tartar in the top of a double boiler over medium heat and whisk for 3 minutes or until warm and the sugar has dissolved. Remove from the heat, add the schnapps and, using electric beater, beat for 6–7 minutes or until glossy and stiff peaks form.

Transfer to a piping bag fitted with a 1 cm (½ inch) plain nozzle and pipe 2 tablespoons of filling onto half of the cookies. Sandwich with the remaining cookies and roll the sides of the pies in the crushed peppermint candies to coat.

Makes 12

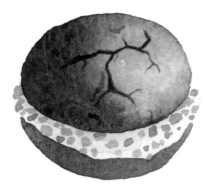

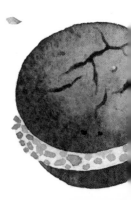

Brownie bites
with
cheesecake topping

125 g (4½ oz) unsalted butter

200 g (7 oz) dark chocolate (70% cocoa solids), finely chopped

220 g (7¾ oz/1 cup) caster (superfine) sugar

3 eggs

150 g (5½ oz/1 cup) plain (all-purpose) flour

1 teaspoon natural vanilla extract

¼ teaspoon salt

cheesecake topping

180 g (6⅓ oz) cream cheese

75 g (2¾ oz/⅓ cup) caster (superfine) sugar

1 egg

1 tablespoon plain (all-purpose) flour

1 teaspoon natural vanilla extract

Preheat the oven to 165°C (320°F/Gas 3).
Grease and line a 27 cm x 17.5 cm
(10¾ inch x 6¾ inch) slice tin with
baking paper.

To make the topping, place the cream
cheese and sugar in the bowl of an electric
mixer and beat on medium speed for
2–3 minutes or until smooth. Add the
egg, flour and vanilla extract and beat to
combine. Transfer to a bowl and set aside.

Place the butter and chocolate in the top
of a double boiler over medium heat and
stir until melted and smooth. Place the sugar
and eggs in the bowl of an electric mixer
and beat for 2 minutes or until light and
creamy. Add the flour, vanilla extract and
salt and beat to combine.

Pour the chocolate mixture into the tin.
Spoon the topping over and spread
evenly. Using a butter knife, cut into the
mixture to create a marbled effect. Bake for
30–35 minutes or until cooked through.
Cool completely in the tin, then slice into
2.5 cm x 2.5 cm (1 inch x 1 inch) bites.

Makes 70

Vanilla cheesecake pops
with
ginger cookie crumbs

40 lollipop sticks

500 g (1 lb 2 oz) white chocolate, melted

125 g (4½ oz) gingersnap biscuits, crushed

vanilla cheesecake

750 g (1 lb 10 oz/3 cups) cream cheese, at room temperature

220 g (7¾ oz/1 cup) caster (superfine) sugar

3 eggs

1 egg yolk

185 g (6½ oz/¾ cup) sour cream

3 tablespoons plain (all-purpose) flour

1 vanilla bean, split and seeds scraped

45 g (1⅔ oz) candied ginger, thinly sliced

To make the cheesecake, preheat the oven to 160°C (315°F/Gas 2–3). Line a 22 cm (8½ inch) round cake tin with baking paper. Place the cream cheese and sugar in the bowl of an electric mixer and beat on medium speed for 1–2 minutes or until smooth and combined. Add the eggs and egg yolk, one at a time, beating well after each addition. Add the sour cream, flour, vanilla seeds and ginger and combine well. Pour into the tin and bake for 1¼ hours or until just set in the centre. Leave in the tin to cool completely, then refrigerate for 3–5 hours or overnight until chilled and very firm.

Line 2 baking trays with baking paper. Using a small ice-cream scoop, scoop balls of cheesecake onto the trays. Quickly roll each in the palm of your hands and shape into a neat ball. Insert a stick into each ball and freeze for 2 hours or until very firm.

Carefully dip each cheesecake pop in the melted chocolate and tap the stick on the side of the bowl while slowly spinning to remove excess chocolate. Roll each pop in the crushed biscuit to coat well. Stand in styrofoam to dry. Serve immediately or store in an airtight container in the refrigerator for 3–4 days.

Makes 35-40

Profiteroles with chocolate-espresso sauce

1 litre (35 fl oz/4 cups) coffee
   ice-cream

profiteroles

125 g (4½ oz) unsalted butter

2 teaspoons caster (superfine) sugar

185 g (6½ oz/1¼ cups) plain
   (all-purpose) flour

4 eggs

chocolate-espresso sauce

150 g (5½ oz) dark chocolate
   (65% cocoa solids), finely
   chopped

55 g (2 oz/¼ cup) caster (superfine)
   sugar

20 g (¾ oz) unsalted butter

125 ml (4½ fl oz/½ cup) thickened
   cream

125 ml (4½ fl oz/½ cup) espresso
   coffee

To make the profiteroles, preheat the oven to 210°C (415°F/Gas 6–7). Line 2 baking trays with baking paper. Place the butter, sugar and 250 ml (9 fl oz/1 cup) water in a saucepan over medium heat and bring to the boil. Add the flour and stir vigorously with a wooden spoon until the dough comes together to form a ball. Continue stirring for 2–3 minutes, then remove from the heat. Transfer to the bowl of an electric mixer fitted with a paddle attachment. Add the eggs, one at a time, beating well after each addition.

Transfer the warm dough to a large piping bag fitted with a 1 cm (½ inch) plain nozzle and pipe 2.5 cm–3 cm (1 inch–1¼ inch) rounds about 2.5 cm (1 inch) apart onto the trays. Bake for 15 minutes, then reduce the heat to 180°C (350°F/ Gas 4) and bake for a further 7–10 minutes. To test if the profiteroles are cooked, cut one in half; it should be hollow and dry inside, not eggy. Cool completely on wire racks.

To make the sauce, place all of the ingredients in the top of a double boiler over medium heat and stir until the chocolate has melted and the sugar has dissolved. Remove from the heat and keep warm.

To serve, halve each profiterole. Using a small ice-cream scoop, scoop out balls of ice-cream and place on the profiterole bases. Sandwich with the tops and drizzle with the sauce.

Makes about 48-50

Raspberry macarons
with
white chocolate

120 g (4¼ oz) almond meal (ground almonds)

220 g (7¾ oz) icing (confectioners') sugar

110 g (3¾ oz) eggwhite

30 g (1 oz) caster (superfine) sugar

2 teaspoons natural raspberry extract

pink food colouring, paste or powdered is preferable

white chocolate ganache

120 g (4¼ oz) white chocolate, chopped

2½ tablespoons pouring (single) cream

2 teaspoons natural raspberry extract

3 teaspoons raspberry jam

Line 2 baking trays with baking paper. Process the almond meal and icing sugar in a food processor until combined, then sift twice. Place the eggwhite in the bowl of an electric mixer and beat on medium speed until frothy, then increase the speed while gradually adding the caster sugar. Continue beating until stiff peaks form, then mix in the raspberry extract and enough colouring for desired effect. Fold one-third into the almond mixture and combine well. Gently fold through the remaining eggwhite mixture; it should be glossy and thick, not thin and runny.

Transfer to a piping bag fitted with a 5 mm (¼ inch) plain nozzle and pipe 3 cm (1¼ inch) circles about 3 cm (1¼ inches) apart onto the trays. Leave at room temperature for 1–6 hours (depending on the humidity) or until a crust forms; the macarons should no longer be sticky to the touch.

Preheat the oven to 140°C (275°F/Gas 1). Bake the macarons for 15–18 minutes until they rise slightly. Immediately slide the macarons and paper off the trays and onto wire racks to cool completely.

Meanwhile, to make the ganache, place the chocolate and cream in the top of a double boiler over medium heat and stir until melted and smooth. Refrigerate for 25–35 minutes or until firm but pliable. Add the raspberry extract and jam and mix well.

Transfer to a small piping bag fitted with a 1 cm (½ inch) plain nozzle and pipe about 1 teaspoon onto half of the macarons. Sandwich with the remaining macarons.

Makes about 30

Dulce de leche cupcakes

185 g (6½ oz/1¼ cups) plain (all-purpose) flour

¾ teaspoon baking powder

2½ teaspoons ground cinnamon, plus extra, for dusting

125 g (4½ oz) unsalted butter, at room temperature

185 g (6½ oz/1 cup lightly packed) soft brown sugar

2 eggs

125 ml (4½ fl oz/½ cup) buttermilk

1 teaspoon natural vanilla extract

125 ml (4½ fl oz/½ cup) dulce de leche (see note)

dulce de leche frosting

125 g (4½ oz) unsalted butter, at room temperature

375 g (13 oz/3 cups) icing (confectioners') sugar

3 tablespoons pouring (single) cream

2 teaspoons natural vanilla extract

125 ml (4½ fl oz/½ cup) dulce de leche (see note)

Preheat the oven to 180°C (350°F/Gas 4). Line 42 x 30 ml (1 fl oz/⅛ cup) capacity mini-muffin holes with paper cases.

To make the cupcakes, sift the flour, baking powder and cinnamon together into a bowl.

Place the butter and sugar in the bowl of an electric mixer and beat on medium speed for 2–3 minutes or until light and creamy. Add the eggs, one at a time, beating well after each addition. Add the flour mixture, in two batches, alternating with the buttermilk, scraping down the sides of the bowl as required. Add the vanilla extract and combine well.

Transfer the batter to a large piping bag fitted with a 1 cm (½ inch) plain nozzle and pipe into the cases, filling them three-quarters full. Bake for 10–12 minutes or until light golden and they spring back lightly to the touch. Cool in the tins for 1–2 minutes, then turn out onto wire racks to cool completely.

Fill a piping bag fitted with a small plain nozzle tip with the dulce de leche. Insert the nozzle into each cupcake and pipe a little dulce de leche into the centre.

To make the frosting, place the butter, icing sugar, cream and vanilla extract in the bowl of an electric mixer and beat on medium speed for 3–4 minutes. Increase the speed to high and beat until light and creamy. Reduce the speed, add the dulce de leche and beat to combine. Transfer to a large piping bag fitted with a small star nozzle and pipe onto the cupcakes. Dust with the extra cinnamon.

Note: Dulce de leche is available from Latin American grocers and gourmet food shops.

Makes 42

Double chocolate whoopie pies

150 g (5½ oz/1 cup) plain (all-purpose) flour

60 g (2¼ oz/½ cup) cocoa powder

½ teaspoon bicarbonate of soda (baking soda)

145 g (5¼ oz/⅔ cup) caster (superfine) sugar

90 g (3¼ oz) unsalted butter, at room temperature

1 teaspoon natural vanilla extract

1 egg

250 ml (9 fl oz/1 cup) milk

chocolate buttercream

3 eggwhites

145 g (5¼ oz/⅔ cup) caster (superfine) sugar

160 g (5⅔ oz) unsalted butter, cubed and at room temperature

125 g (4½ oz) dark chocolate (65% cocoa solids), melted

2 tablespoons cocoa powder

Preheat the oven to 175°C (340°F/Gas 3–4). Grease and flour 2 baking trays or 3 whoopie pie tins. Sift the flour, cocoa and bicarbonate of soda together into a large bowl. Place the sugar and butter in the bowl of an electric mixer and beat on medium speed for 2–3 minutes or until light and creamy. Add the vanilla extract and egg and beat for a further minute. Reduce the speed and add the flour mixture, in three batches, alternating with the milk and beat until combined, scraping down the sides of the bowl as required.

Place 1½ tablespoon amounts of batter about 5 cm (2 inches) apart on the trays and bake for 8–10 minutes or until cooked through. Cool for 5 minutes on the trays, then transfer to wire racks to cool completely.

Meanwhile, to make the buttercream, place the eggwhites and sugar in the top of a double boiler over medium heat and whisk for 3–4 minutes or until warm and the sugar has dissolved. Remove from the heat. Using electric beaters, beat the mixture on medium–high speed for 6–7 minutes or until glossy and stiff peaks form. Reduce the speed and add the butter, one cube at a time, beating well after each addition. Continue to beat for 2–3 minutes. Combine the melted chocolate and cocoa. Add to the eggwhite mixture and beat to combine.

Transfer to a piping bag fitted with a 1 cm (½ inch) plain nozzle and pipe 2 tablespoons of filling onto half of the cookies. Sandwich with the remaining cookies.

Makes 12

Raspberry cupcakes
with
white chocolate ganache

96 fresh raspberries

150 g (5½ oz) white chocolate, finely
   chopped

120 g (4¼ oz) unsalted butter

85 g (3 oz) caster (superfine) sugar

125 ml (4½ fl oz/½ cup) milk

125 g (4½ oz) plain (all-purpose) flour

½ teaspoon baking powder

1 egg, lightly beaten

½ teaspoon natural vanilla extract

100 g (3½ oz) white chocolate, for
   decoration

white chocolate ganache

180 g (6⅓ oz) white chocolate,
   finely chopped

400 ml (14 fl oz) pouring (single)
   cream

To make the ganache, place the chocolate and cream in the top of a double
boiler over medium heat and stir until melted and smooth. Transfer to a bowl and
refrigerate for 20 minutes. Remove and stir, then refrigerate for a further 20 minutes.
Repeat the process twice more. (At this point, the ganache can be covered and
refrigerated overnight.)

Meanwhile, preheat the oven to 150°C (300°F/Gas 2). Line 48 x 30 ml (1 fl oz/⅛ cup) capacity mini-muffin holes with paper cases and place one raspberry in the base of each.

Place the chocolate, butter, sugar and milk in the top of a double boiler over medium heat and stir until melted and smooth. Leave to cool for 15 minutes.

Sift the flour and baking powder together into a large bowl. Add the chocolate mixture and stir to combine. Add the egg and vanilla extract and mix well. The batter should be quite runny.

Transfer to a jug and pour into the cases, filling them three-quarters full. Bake for 11–12 minutes or until cooked. Cool in the tins for 3–5 minutes, then turn out onto wire racks to cool completely.

Transfer the ganache to the bowl of an electric mixer and beat on medium speed for 1–2 minutes or until soft peaks form. Transfer to a large piping bag fitted with a small star nozzle and pipe swirls of ganache onto each cupcake. Top each with a raspberry and, using a vegetable peeler, shave over curls of chocolate.

Makes 48

Index

Published in 2012 by Hardie Grant Books

Hardie Grant Books (Australia)
Ground Floor, Building 1
658 Church Street
Richmond, Victoria 3121
www.hardiegrant.com.au

Hardie Grant Books (UK)
Dudley House, North Suite
34–35 Southampton Street
London WC2E 7HF

National Library of Australia Cataloguing-in-Publication Data available

ISBN 9781742702919

Publisher Paul McNally
Editor Belinda So
Design manager Heather Menzies
Designed and illustrated by Daniella Germain
Recipes written by Deborah Kaloper
Production Penny Sanderson

NB: The recipes in *Sweetie!* first appeared in *Bitesize: macarons, cake pops and cute things*

Colour reproduction by Splitting Image Colour Studio
Printed in China by 1010 Printing International Limited

COLLINS

ENGLISH SPRINGER
SPANIEL

AN OWNER'S GUIDE

The authors

Yvonne Billows, together with her husband Ron, has successfully bred and exhibited English Springer Spaniels for over 20 years. Based in Cheshire, their Robil kennel has produced five Show Champions. They are both top-level judges of the breed, qualified to award Challenge Certificates at British Championship Shows and CACIBs at International Championship Shows. Yvonne also judges all breeds at Open Show level.

A founder member of the Lancashire and Cheshire English Springer Spaniel Club, Yvonne holds the position of Honorary Secretary and organises two shows each year. She has successfully produced and delivered a seminar on judging the breed for The English Springer Spaniel Club. On a professional level, Yvonne is employed in a training/counselling environment. She is a member of the Institute of Internal Auditors and the BAC, and also has a diploma in counselling.

John Bower BVSc, MRCVS is a senior partner in a small animal Veterinary Hospital in Plymouth, England. He has served as President of both the British Veterinary Association and the British Small Animal Veterinary Association. He writes regularly for the veterinary press and also for dog and cat publications. He is co-author of two dog healthcare books and a member of the Kennel Club.

Caroline Bower BVM&S, MRCVS runs a veterinary health centre in the same practice as John. Her special interests include prevention and treatment of behavioural problems, and she lectures to dog breeding and training groups.

COLLINS

ENGLISH SPRINGER
SPANIEL
AN OWNER'S GUIDE

Yvonne Billows

HarperCollins*Publishers*

DEDICATION
To Ronnie and my mother Rosalie for being the wind beneath my wings, to Ann J as the best
PA ever, and to Suzette and Brigita for keeping my body and soul together.

First published in 1997 by
HarperCollins*Publishers*
London

A catalogue record of this book is available
from the British Library

ISBN 0 00 412971 7

This book was created by SP Creative Design for HarperCollins*Publishers* Ltd
Editor: Heather Thomas
Designer: Rolando Ugolini
Production: Rolando Ugolini
Illustrations: Al Rockall and Rolando Ugolini

Photography:
François Nicaise: pages 1, 6, 7, 9, 10, 11, 12, 13, 14, 17, 20, 24, 27, 28, 32, 37, 43, 46, 47, 48,
52, 53, 64, 73, 74, 77, 82, 83, 85, 86, 87, 92, 94
David Dalton: pages 3, 5, 11, 13, 16, 19, 21, 31, 33, 34, 35, 36, 39, 40, 41, 42, 43, 45, 49, 50,
54, 55, 56, 58, 59, 60, 61, 62, 63, 65, 66, 67, 68, 69, 70, 71, 72, 79, 80, 88
Sally Anne Thompson: page 18

Acknowledgements
The publishers would like to thank the following for their kind assistance in producing this book:
Scampers School for Dogs for their help with photography, and special thanks to Charlie
Clarricoates for all his hard work.

Ann, Sian and Luke Corbett of the 'Trimere' Kennel with their English Springer Spaniels: Show
Champion Trimere Terrahawk, Show Champion Mompesson Memory Lane and Trimere Treasured
Memory and also their Welsh Springer Spaniel: Show Champion Northey Scarlet Lady at Trimere.

Colour reproduction by Colourscan, Singapore
Printed and bound by New Interlitho SpA, Italy

CONTENTS

PART ONE

YOU AND YOUR DOG

So you're thinking about owning an English Springer Spaniel? I don't blame you – they are the most loving breed one could ever own. I worked in a show Gundog kennels in my youth; that's when I first fell in love with the breed and vowed to own them myself one day. Now, having successfully exhibited, bred and owned them for over 20 years, I'm reasonably qualified to give you my very biased opinion!

I don't look at English Springer Spaniels through rose-tinted glasses all the time and I admit that they do have their little foibles. Throughout this book I have endeavoured to share some of my experiences and have tried to offer realistic help and guidance. If you are new to the breed you need to know what you're about to embark on, and you can benefit from reading this book as an aide to English Springer Spaniel ownership. This will hopefully enable you to secure many happy years of unconditional love and companionship from a perfect family pet.

CHAPTER ONE

HISTORY AND BREED CHARACTERISTICS

SHOW DOGS AND WORKING DOGS

The English Kennel Club Breed Standard for the English Springer Spaniel, which is the approved benchmark against which all dogs are assessed, has been around since the beginning of the twentieth century. It advises that 'the breed is of ancient and pure origins, oldest of the sporting Gundogs, whose original purpose was finding and springing game for the net, falcon or greyhound. Now used to find, flush and retrieve game for gun.'

If you are new to the English Springer Spaniel, you may not know that whilst it is initially one breed of dog, the mid-twentieth century saw it beginning to divide into two distinct lines. Although their looks differ somewhat, they still manage to meet the Breed Standard in their own individual way. These two lines are generally known today as:

■ The Show English Springer Spaniel
■ The Working English Springer Spaniel

Briefly, the show line is bigger than the working line, with heavier bones and a slightly different shape to the dome of the head, ear set and length, and muzzle. Many people believe that the show line is more aesthetically pleasing but whilst both types of English Springer have the instinct to work and can be trained to the gun, the working line is generally thought to be much keener, quicker and stylish in its results.

Whenever a person without any knowledge of our lovely breed tells me that they would like an English Springer, I always ask the question, 'Do you know about the different lines and which one you want?' Most novices I have met don't know, and they very often say that they only want a Springer for a pet, and not for showing or working. However, puppies from both lines can make excellent pets, as not all of them will do well in the ring as a show dog or in the field as a worker. The nature of the split can be quite confusing, so it is helpful to clarify some breed history details.

English Springer Spaniels are the oldest of all the sporting gundogs.

HISTORY OF THE BREED

From the name 'Spaniel' it is generally believed that the many different types originated in Great Britain, having been introduced from Spain by the Romans. Specialist history books on the breed state that the term 'Springing Spaniel' was not given initially to a particular breed of Spaniel, but was used merely to describe the action of all types of Spaniels that sprang game. Some of these were the varieties we now know as Clumber, Cocker, Sussex, Field, English and Welsh Springers, although in the early days, all types of Spaniel were not as pure as we know them today.

English Springer Spaniel enthusiasts owe a debt of gratitude to the Boughey family of Shropshire. In approximately 1800 they developed a distinct strain of 'Springer Spaniel', which was bred very carefully, and from 1813 onwards they kept meticulous records to ensure that

This working English Springer Spaniel is retrieving a bird. Springers find, flush and retrieve game.

valuable information was available for breeders to keep the strain pure. Records confirm that this strain was kept by the Boughey family for well over 100 years.

Around 1902, the Kennel Club recognised English and Welsh Springer Spaniels as separate breeds and dogs were registered with them according to which Breed Standard they most closely resembled. Registration was not compulsory and some breeders carried on breeding and showing from their unregistered stock – something that would not be allowed today. The Kennel Club also gave the breed its own classes at Dog Shows and a few years later, in 1906, the first Champion English Springer Spaniel was crowned – a liver and white dog called Beechgrove Will.

Springers have strong characters and are always eager to please.

In 1913, a dog called Rivington Sam became the first English Springer Spaniel to become a Field Trial Champion. Although this was a long time ago, it is generally believed that most of our present-day stock originates from him.

Once the breed had become firmly

The handsome Welsh Springer Spaniel was recognised around 1902 as a separate breed from the English Springer.

English Springers are friendly dogs with a biddable temperament.

today and plays a major part in both show and field trial circles. Since the time of their inception, nine other breed clubs and societies throughout the UK have been recognised by the Kennel Club. However, the English Springer Spaniel Club is still fondly known as 'the parent club' (for details of the breed clubs, see page 144).

The two lines

However, interest in the breed was to split and, during the middle of this century, it began to divide into two distinct lines with looks that differed somewhat. Owners began to breed their English Springer Spaniels for particular looks and characteristics depending on which line they wished to concentrate on – this type of breeding programme is still followed today and most serious breeders do not mix the lines. As already stated, these two lines are known as the Show English Springer Spaniel and the Working English Springer Spaniel, and although looks differ to a certain degree, they still conform to the same Breed Standard.

Once you decide which line of English Springer you are interested in, any Breed Club Secretary should be able to advise you who to approach for the different lines.

established it was quickly recognised that it could do much more than spring game. It could do the work of all the other Gundogs in so far as it could hunt, point the game, spring and retrieve it, whilst being unperturbed by thick brambles and deep water. It became known as a veritable handyman, able to perform equally well in both the showring and the field, and its popularity went from strength to strength. So much so that in 1921 the Kennel Club approved the registration of 'The English Springer Spaniel Club' with a committee made up of both show and field trial owners. This club is still very much in evidence

WORKING AND SHOW TYPE

You can see from studying these two photographs the physical differences between the working English Springer Spaniel and the show-type dog. The working line (right) is smaller than the show line (above), with lighter bones and a slightly different shape to the dome of the head, ear set and length, and muzzle. Although the show line is considered more aesthetically pleasing, both dogs make wonderful pets and loyal companions.

THE BREED STANDARD

Reproduced with kind permission of the Kennel Club

General Appearance Symmetrically built, compact, strong, merry, active. Highest on leg and raciest in build of all British land Spaniels.

Characteristics Breed is of ancient and pure origins, oldest of sporting gundogs; original purpose was finding and springing game for net, falcon or greyhound. Now used to find, flush and retrieve game for gun.

Size Approximate height: 51 cms (20 ins).

Tail Set low, never carried above level of back. Well feathered with lively action. Customarily docked.

Hindquarters Hindlegs well let down. Stifles and hocks moderately bent. Thighs broad, muscular, well developed. Coarse hocks undesirable.

Gait/Movement Strictly his own. Forelegs swing straight forward from shoulder, throwing feet well forward in an easy free manner. Hocks driving well under body, following in line with forelegs. At slow movement may have a pacing stride typical of this breed.

Temperament Friendly, happy disposition, biddable. Timidity or aggression highly undesirable.

Body Strong, neither too long nor too short. Chest deep, well developed. Well sprung ribs. Loin muscular, strong with slight arch and well coupled.

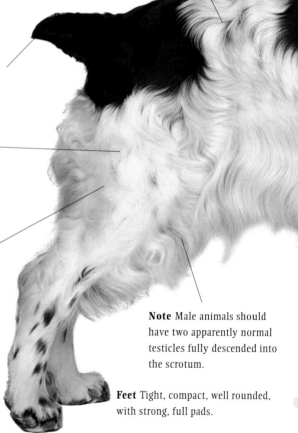

Note Male animals should have two apparently normal testicles fully descended into the scrotum.

Feet Tight, compact, well rounded, with strong, full pads.

Eyes Medium size, almond-shaped, not prominent nor sunken, well set in (not showing haw), alert, kind expression. Dark hazel. Light eyes undesirable.

Mouth Jaws strong, with a perfect, regular and complete scissor bite, i.e. upper teeth closely overlapping lower teeth and set square to the jaws.

Head and Skull Skull of medium length, fairly broad, slightly rounded, rising from foreface, making a brow or stop, divided by fluting between eyes, dying away along forehead towards occipital bone which should not be prominent. Cheeks flat. Foreface of proportionate length to skull, fairly broad and deep, well chiselled below eyes, fairly deep and square in flew. Nostrils well developed.

Neck Good length, strong and muscular, free from throatiness, slightly arched, tapering towards head.

Ears Lobular, good length and width, fairly close to head, set in line with eye. Nicely feathered.

Coat Close, straight and weather resisting, never coarse. Moderate feathering on ears, forelegs, body and hindquarters.

Colour Liver and white, black and white, or either of these colours with tan markings.

Forequarters Forelegs straight and well boned. Shoulders sloping and well laid. Elbows well to body. Strong flexible pasterns.

Faults Any departure from the foregoing points should be considered a fault and the seriousness with which the fault should be regarded should be in exact proportion to its degree.

CHAPTER TWO

BEHAVIOUR

PETS AND WORKING DOGS

The English Springer Spaniel is a very loving dog, and a favourite for joining family life. Kennel Club statistics reveal that it is usually in the top five most popular Gundog breeds in the UK; this fact also reflects the Springer's popularity in the show ring and as a very versatile working gundog.

Social and Working Partners

English Springer Spaniels have been used as working gundogs for many years.

Nowadays, we have also learnt to accord them a new status as our social and working partners and the breed is recognised for its versatility and talents. There is no doubt that this is due to an intelligent and biddable temperament, and a strong character which is always eager

English Springer Spaniels are popular companions on a day's shoot. They make very successful working gundogs, retrieving game.

to please. Their multi-skills mean we now see Springers in many other roles.

- They are successful in obedience competitions.
- They are successful in agility competitions.
- They are used as PAT dogs (this is active therapy, whereby an owner takes the dog to visit children or the elderly in homes and hospitals, in order to aid recovery or bring a purpose to life).
- They are used as Hearing Dogs for the

Working Springers will willingly take to the water to retrieve game. They are versatile dogs, making good pets as well as hard-working gundogs.

Deaf (whereby the dogs are trained to be the ears of their owners and to alert them to noises such as the doorbell and telephone).

- They have been used successfully as sniffer dogs in detection work with the Customs and Excise, police, armed forces

and prison service (working with drugs and explosives).

■ They feature as photographic models (for example, on greetings cards and advertisements).

■ A Springer has even been an author! Millie Bush, the English Springer belonging to the American President George Bush, published her own book about life in the White House.

Perfect family pets

Research undertaken regarding the perfect family pet, looked at categories of behaviour from excitability to snappiness, and from basic obedience to dominance over the owner. The study was carried out with the intention of supplying vets with information that would help them to advise their clients on the most suitable dog for differing lifestyles.

As one would expect, there were dramatic differences between the breeds in the survey. However, the English Springer Spaniel came out in the group with the best score and closest to being the perfect family pet. This group scored low on aggression (i.e. has a good temperament) and was about average in reactions to its surroundings (i.e. can adapt to most situations). The only disadvantage was that dogs in this group were judged to be very immature – in other words, they tend to go on thinking that they are puppies for most of their lives! Lovers of the English Springer are likely to tell you that they do not see this as a drawback, more a bonus as they are always ready and willing

Springer Spaniels are energetic dogs and need a lot of exercise. They are good family pets and get on well with children.

to have fun and give their owners lots of pleasure over the years.

Foibles and peculiarities

Most long-time owners of English Springer Spaniels are well and truly hooked on the breed. When they lose one through old age, they will always replace it with another English Springer Spaniel, often returning to the breeder of their first dog. However, even people who love the breed dearly are the first to admit that English Springers have their little foibles and peculiarities. Here are a few of the more common ones.

■ They think they are human and want to do everything you do – and I mean everything!

■ They develop the art of turning into a block of concrete when you are trying to get them some place they don't want to go – such as a visit to the vet.

■ They like to do impressions, such as imitating a pelican. This is when they fill their mouths with as much water as they can carry before seeking you out and kindly putting their head on your knee – just when you've dressed up to go out.

■ They live up to their name and are able to continuously jump up and down using only their back legs, as if they had springs attached to them.

■ They believe that if they can reach something then it must be acceptable for them to have it – home baking, in particular.

THE OWNER AS PACK LEADER

Although our lovely Springers tend to think that they are human, they are, of course, animals with their own special needs and should be treated accordingly so that they know their place in family life.

In the wild, dogs generally live in a pack environment and would have an order of hierarchy in their lives. There would be a dominant leader in the pack who would have to be obeyed. Whilst the English Springer is not from wild stock, the situation is the same for domestic animals. A dog is born with the instinct to form social groups, and, if as a puppy he is brought up with humans, he is likely to treat you and your family as his pack members. It is very important, therefore, that your English Springer

You are the pack leader and your dog should obey your commands as a result of reward-based training and control by your voice.

Spaniel grows up knowing that he is not the leader of the pack – you are. Your dog has to do what you want if you are to ensure a problem-free environment. I have always found that English Springers are quite happy to accept humans in this role.

Your dog should understand that his ranking is below everyone in your family, and that he has to do whatever he is told. Through a praise and reward training system and control by tone of voice alone, your ultimate aim is that your dog will learn to trust and respect you.

Problem behaviour

The most common situation I come across when someone experiences problem behaviour from a dog of any breed, is the owner who says 'My dog doesn't like being brushed so we don't do it' or 'We can't go out because the dog doesn't like being left on his own' or even 'Once my dog gets on the chair he growls when we tell him to get off, so we leave him there!' These are clear examples of a dog exerting his authority and being allowed to get away with it. This kind of behaviour is something that should never be allowed to start.

Antisocial behaviour

There are other aspects of antisocial behaviour, both from the point of view of the dog and the owner, which apply to all dogs, not just the English Springer Spaniel. Some quite common examples of this are as follows:

- Dogs running loose on the roads – this is bad ownership and one wonders why such people bother to have a dog. By his nature, a domestic dog relies on a human to provide food, shelter, warmth and affection, and consequently may frighten a non-dog lover when he goes off wandering in search of these things.
- Dog faeces in a public place – this means anywhere outside your home. Responsible dog owners clean up after

You should teach your dog to gently take food out of your hand rather than snatching at it.

their dogs so that the faeces cannot contaminate other humans.

■ Prolonged barking – this usually happens when the dog has been left

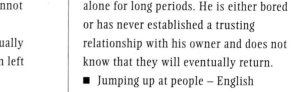

alone for long periods. He is either bored or has never established a trusting relationship with his owner and does not know that they will eventually return.

■ Jumping up at people – English Springers are very friendly dogs and will always welcome you, your family and friends enthusiastically. When the dog is small it seems alright to let this type of behaviour go; but when he is fully grown and weighs about 22 kg (50 lb) you will definitely regret it.

■ Snatching food from your hand – this can happen, of course, with any breed and is especially dangerous when young children are about.

■ Correct training, combined with a solid routine begun at an early age, should eliminate all these types of antisocial behaviour. There is a lot of truth in the old saying that 'there is no such thing as a bad dog, only a bad owner'.

Jumping up at people should be discouraged from an early age. Don't let your puppy establish bad habits and antisocial behaviour.

PART TWO

CARING FOR YOUR DOG

Buying any puppy or acquiring an adult dog is a huge responsibility, and caring for any dog will take up a lot of your time over the next ten or so years. Therefore it is not a decision to be taken lightly but one that requires careful consideration by all the members of your family. Small Springer puppies can look especially appealing but they should never be bought on impulse. Many people forget that these cute little creatures grow up into large dogs. English Springer Spaniels make good companions and loving family pets but, as with all large breeds, they need a great deal of exercise and lots of your attention. In this section on caring for your dog, you will find expert advice on choosing a puppy and looking after him; feeding, exercising and grooming your adult dog; and also how you can both enjoy the experience of showing your dog.

Chapter Three

The English Springer Spaniel Puppy

Buying a Puppy

Getting an English Springer Spaniel puppy is a bit like becoming a parent – life is never the same again. All domestic routines and relationships have to change to accommodate the physical and psychological requirements of this small, but demanding, being. So, when a potential English Springer Spaniel owner comes to see our dogs, with a view to purchasing a puppy, we talk for a couple of hours about everything that will be involved to ensure a successful ownership.

You must think about the following considerations before you take a decision and set out to buy your puppy. Consider each area, and when you're sure that you have addressed all the issues effectively, that's probably the best time to start the wheels in motion for obtaining your English Springer Spaniel.

Your commitment

An English Springer Spaniel puppy is a living thing which will be around for a long time, with an average lifespan of about fourteen years. Think about whether you are willing to commit yourself to being a responsible pet owner for the whole of your dog's life. One of the joys of dog ownership is simply being in charge of a healthy good-looking animal. This sort of pride is quite justified, as taking care of a dog can be demanding. However, a much admired animal, together with the known benefits that playing with your dog can bring (i.e. helping you relax and unwind after a hard day's work) are a fair reward for all the time, expense and effort that you will expend throughout your dog's life.

Your lifestyle and available time

English Springers can make excellent companions but they do require you to

An English Springer puppy may look very appealing but you must never buy one on impulse. Only get a puppy after careful consideration of the advantages and disadvantages of owning a dog. And only buy from a recognised breeder – not from a pet shop or a puppy farm.

All puppies love to play and to explore.

dedicate a lot of time to their upbringing and training. It may even be necessary to re-think the style of your home and garden if you are rather houseproud or a particularly keen gardener.

English Springers could also affect your social life, as you should not leave any dog on its own for long periods. You

EXPENSE

Have you thought about how much the initial outlay of expense will be and whether you can afford to buy a puppy? A quick phone call to your nearest breed club will give you an idea of how much a puppy will cost (see the list of addresses on page 144). You will also have to include the cost of feeding bowls, a dog bed, a collar and lead, toys, grooming equipment and vaccinations.

Weekly costs will include a good-quality food and any vets' bills that are incurred for preventative treatment. You may also want to consider one of the many good pet insurances on the market, which will take the sting out of any large vets' bills, and also third-party liability insurance. Most vets' surgeries will have details of the policies that are available to you.

might need to consider if particular arrangements need to be made if ever you have to be away from home for long. It is advisable for anyone who works full time to think twice about getting a puppy unless adequate arrangements can be made to provide a caring, effective 'nannying' service until the pup becomes a young adult (this is in the interests of both the well-being of your dog and your home remaining intact).

Timing

You also need to consider the right time for you to get the puppy – this should be well thought out and the puppy should definitely not be bought on impulse. Once you have bought your puppy, you will need some dedicated time to settle him into your home, so don't acquire him at Christmas or just before you go on holiday. One last thing: whilst English Springer Spaniels make wonderful pets, they are not suitable for a person who is housebound or infirm as they need a lot of exercise and attention, especially when young.

Size and space

English Springers generally grow to about 50 cm (20 in) high at the shoulder and are strong animals weighing around 22 kg (50 lb). What is more, they are always full of energy. Have a look around where you live and decide whether you really have sufficient space for a Springer. They are definitely not suitable for flat dwellers or people without some kind of securely fenced garden or outside area.

Where will your dog live? He will certainly need his own space in the house – somewhere for his bed to be kept permanently and where he can freely go when he wants to sleep. I am a firm believer that if a dog is bought as a pet, he should live in the home and not outside in a kennel. Most breeders want to be sure that any new owner buying a puppy from them would be planning to treat him as one of the family.

Exercise

Exercising your English Springer Spaniel every day is essential and can also be very beneficial to your own health – but do you have the time to do this and is your present state of health up to it? Is where you live conducive to exercising a dog? Dogs should never be let out of your home to exercise themselves. This is inexcusable and the sort of behaviour that gives all dog owners a bad name. It is more than likely to result in both the animal and other human beings getting hurt at some stage.

Whose responsibility?

More often than not, this is the one area on which most families cannot agree. One thing is for sure (and it's one of my own special conditions that potential puppy owners have to satisfy) and that is that every member of the family really has to want the dog and must be willing to take responsibility for him, including the tasks listed opposite:

While your Springer is a puppy, he should have only limited exercise. However, adult dogs need a daily run.

long hair on their chest, legs and underbelly. All this needs to be regularly groomed and kept free from knots. Your dog's teeth and ears also need to be checked and cleaned regularly.

■ **Cleaning up dog faeces** – this is likely to be the least favourite task but it should be done every time the dog leaves you with this kind of 'present'. It is unavoidable and the task comes with every dog! This also includes mopping up the inevitable and numerous puddles your puppy is likely to make until he is house-trained.

■ **Feeding** – regular feeding, washing the dishes and making sure that clean water in a clean bowl is always available.

■ **Tidying up after the pup** – this may mean picking up the pieces of newspaper he has just chewed, mopping the kitchen floor to remove muddy footprints and vacuuming the dog hairs off the carpet.

■ **Grooming** – English Springers have beautiful, long, well-feathered ears and lots of

A Springer's coat needs regular grooming and should be kept free of knots.

DOG OR BITCH – WHICH DO YOU CHOOSE?

The temperament of an English Springer Spaniel is such that it probably does not matter which sex you choose. Provided that you train your dog properly you will have no problems as Springers are very loving animals. Dogs, by their nature, are slightly bigger and stronger than bitches and, unless trained properly, they can sometimes be a little headstrong. However, they do not come into season (on heat) as bitches do.

A bitch will first come into season at around six to twelve months of age and then usually every six months after that. The season lasts about three weeks and during that time the bitch will have a discharge of blood. This usually starts off quite light and then darkens up in colour, going back to a light discharge towards the

Puppies enjoy a game and a rough and tumble outside in the garden.

end of the season. A bitch usually cleans herself during this time and you may not always be aware of the discharge at the time. However, she will be emitting a very attractive scent during these three weeks and may draw some unwanted admirers; a state of cautiousness is therefore required at this time, as it is during her season that she can be mated by a dog.

If you choose a bitch as a pet with no intention of breeding from her, it is advisable to have her spayed at an early age, thus eliminating the season and also, of course, any unwanted pregnancies. Veterinary research has shown that early spaying can reduce the risk of mammary tumours, too. Spaying also prevents your bitch suffering from pyometra which is a serious and life-threatening infection of the womb.

There are two old wives' tales that spring to mind here. One says that it is much kinder to let a bitch have a litter – this is definitely false. The other states that spaying makes a bitch fat – if your bitch puts on extra weight then you should reduce her

diet accordingly. One last thing you may like to know if you are a keen gardener: grass is likely to discolour if bitches urinate on the same spot so a disciplined approach will be needed when house-training your puppy.

A puppy or an older dog?

Most people choose to buy a puppy at around eight weeks of age and they are prepared to rear and train him, but you might like to consider an older dog. By older, I mean that he could be an older puppy, a young adult or even an older adult. Breeders, who also show their dogs, may have kept the two best puppies in the litter to rear together. At the point at which they make up their minds as to which one to keep, the other puppy is likely to be for sale; this could be anything up to about six months old.

You may also find a young dog originally kept for the show ring for sale; he may have been shown a few times and

CHILDREN AND SPRINGERS

English Springer Spaniels generally have wonderful temperaments, especially if purchased from reputable breeders. Therefore, they will be superb with children and, no doubt, great friendships will be forged. Psychologists inform us that as children are growing up they tell their dogs secrets they would never dream of sharing with anyone else, and this can sometimes help a child make sense of life. Owning a dog can be a useful social asset and help the child to develop self confidence and friendships.

Dogs also allow children to learn about the responsibility of ownership and can serve as a useful introduction to the experiences of life and death. Having said all of this, children do need to realise that a puppy is not a toy, but a living animal which needs to be treated as such. Very small children may find this difficult to understand and can try the patience of the most loving puppy. For this reason, it is recommended that, unless you have plenty of time and patience, you don't obtain a puppy (of any breed) whilst you have very small children at the crawling and toddling stage.

not turned out to be what the breeder wants. In both these instances you are likely to get a very well reared and loving puppy, which may have been trained, and could have

already passed through the teething stage.

You may also be considering giving an older dog a home and this could be due to the same circumstances. If you live in the UK, you might like to know about the work that the English Springer Spaniel 'Rescue' and 'Welfare' does. These two organisations are run by volunteers, whose objective is to re-home unwanted English Springers who have been someone's pet. The need for re-homing is usually due to no fault of the dog. Volunteers from 'Rescue' and 'Welfare' take great pains to place the right dog in the right home, at the right time and this involves them vetting potential owners. This may be something you want to find out more about and the addresses can be found at the end of this book (see page 144).

ACQUIRING A SPRINGER

The decision is made – the time is right for you to get an English Springer Spaniel; but where from? You've done all your homework, made some decisions and you are now ready. I have geared this chapter to you buying a puppy or a young adult. If you decide to buy an older dog or take one from 'Rescue' or 'Welfare', you should draw whatever information you need from this chapter and the one on 'The Adult Dog'.

Finding a breeder

You should always go to a reputable breeder – an expert in their field. You will be able to find out from one of the English Springer Spaniel breed clubs and societies which breeder has puppies available. You should make it known for what purpose you want your dog (whether it be solely as a pet, for working with, or for the show ring) and ensure that you are referred to the right breeder.

There may be a waiting list, and you might even have to order a puppy – but for such an important addition to your family, it is worth waiting for the right dog. In the UK, the Kennel Club Registrations Department may also be able to tell you who has stock for sale.

CAUTION

Never buy a puppy from a so-called 'puppy farm'. This is where there are many breeds of puppies available (a bit like a supermarket). These ventures are usually money-making concerns and the rearing and welfare of the puppy may not be their first and foremost objective.

Evidence of good temperament

Always try and see the mother (the dam) and her puppies together as this will give you some indication of how the puppies will grow up. It is not always possible when buying a puppy to see the pup's father (the sire) as he may belong to another owner.

A word of warning here: never take children with you if you are going to look at a litter; not unless you're sure that you won't crack under the emotional pressure of being persuaded by the children to take the first little bundle of fluff that you see. A reputable breeder won't mind you making more than one visit and you can take the children with you the second time you go along.

Don't be upset if you are vetted by the breeder with a view to being a potential owner. Responsible breeders do care about where their puppies are going and what happens to them. In fact, most reputable breeders will insist that, if for any reason you find you cannot keep your dog, you must contact them to assist in re-homing him (these things can happen, due to sickness, death, divorce, etc.).

Your puppy should not be timid or aggressive, and he should respond readily to love and affection.

Choosing a puppy

You should be aware that if a breeder has bred a litter with the purpose of keeping a puppy for breeding or showing, it is possible that they will not make their choice until the pups are about eight weeks of age, sometimes even later. Therefore, you are not likely to be told which one you can have until quite late on, and then it's up to you whether you accept it. One thing is for certain: there should be no sub-standard puppies as they will all have been reared with the same love and attention as if the breeder was keeping them all. Logically, if the breeder does not know which pup they intend to keep, then all the litter will have been brought up in the same way. Puppies grow and change so fast in the early stages of their lives that it is a difficult task to decide which is the best from the breeder's point of view.

WHAT TO LOOK FOR

■ Whatever happens, the puppy you end up with should be a happy one, with a wet nose, clear eyes which are not runny, and a well covered body (i.e. not skin and bone).

■ The coat should be clean, soft, shiny and free from sores. Cleanliness may be difficult to assess if the pups are in an outside run and it's been raining, or if they have just been fed and have been playing and rolling in their dinner – a whole host of puppies at dinner time is a sight to behold.

■ Don't make your choice instantly – sit for a while to watch how the puppies interact with each other and find out who the characters are. This will allow you to get some insight into how they have been reared and you will be able to make a decision as to whether one of these pups is right for you.

All young puppies look adorable but you should always choose a healthy one.

PLANNING FOR YOUR PUPPY'S ARRIVAL

There are things you need to do, and obtain, in advance of your puppy's arrival so that he can be integrated quickly into your home life. These are as follows:

- Making contact with a vet
- Jobs around the house
- Obtaining the essentials

Making contact with a vet

You should make enquiries to find a reputable vet in the area, who can advise you on all aspects of canine health, including vaccinations and a routine worming programme. One of the most important reasons for striking up a close relationship with a vet is that he will often be able to work with you in a preventative capacity to help stop things going wrong in your dog's life – similar to a health check for us!

Vets usually like to see their patients at the practice and this is much more cost effective for you than home visits. If you have an emergency outside surgery hours and telephone the vet, you will usually find that he will arrange to meet you at the surgery right away (as it is there that the best means can be found to treat your pet). Most vets will tell you that if you think your dog

JOBS AROUND THE HOUSE

There are a few things you might want to look at in your home before the puppy arrives. Because a puppy has no sense of judgement, and will therefore not know what is and isn't safe, you need to look at what might cause him harm and what needs to be done to protect him. Think extra hard about places around your home, as many English Springers like to think that they are related to Houdini. For example, you may need to do the following things.

- Mend any holes in fences and put locks on gates to stop the puppy getting out of your garden.
- Block up gaps behind garden sheds, cookers, fridges and washing machines – it is no use complaining when you have to dismantle the whole thing to release a puppy who is stuck behind it.
- Make safe any loose or trailing electrical cables that the puppy might chew.
- Put all harmful garden chemicals and paint-type substances in a safe place where they cannot be reached.
- You will also find that all members of the family suddenly start to put things away when a puppy arrives. There's nothing like seeing one of your best shoes in shreds on the kitchen floor to teach you a valuable lesson in tidiness.

has an infectious disease, you should leave him in the car until you are called for your appointment. It is usually a good idea to take your puppy to the vet in the first few days of ownership. The reasons for this are three-fold.

■ The vet will give your puppy a health check and, hopefully, reassure you that your purchase was a good one.

■ You will be given some worming tablets for the puppy, told how and when to administer them and the importance of doing this regularly. Given that your puppy's health could be at risk, it is always best to use products supplied by the vet and not bought over the shop counter.

■ The vet will be able to start your puppy on a course of vaccinations. These are preventative vaccinations for possible life-threatening illnesses to your dog. It is extremely important that your puppy should not mix with any other dogs outside the home until he has completed his primary course of vaccinations. The number and timing of the injections will depend on the age at which your puppy starts the course, and your vet will advise you on the exact details.

Obtaining the essentials

■ Dog bed

Decide where it is going to go (a warm, dry and quiet place) but be prepared to move it a few times if the puppy doesn't like where you put it. The oval-shaped hard plastic beds are quite good as these are washable. I used to think that they couldn't be chewed, but I now know different – English Springers can chew through anything (we once had a puppy who chewed up a metal comb!). For this reason, I wouldn't bother with a glamorous and expensive woven-style basket until the dog is past the chewing stage. If you can get hold of a strong cardboard box and cut it to the right shape, this will probably suffice whilst the pup is quite small. A piece of vetbed in the box is ideal for the puppy to lie on. You can put newspapers underneath the vetbed; any accidents will then soak into the newspaper and keep the bedding dry.

■ Food and bowls

Ask the breeder before you collect the puppy for information on his diet. Try and stick to the same type of food so as not to upset the pup's stomach. Some breeders will give you a small supply of food with your puppy, which will last for a couple of days. Try and find this out before the big day. If they do not give you any advice, see the section on feeding a puppy later in this chapter (see page 50).

You should also buy a stone water bowl, and fresh water should be made available for the puppy at all times. I

Before you bring your new puppy home, you should invest in a washable bed and some bedding – a plastic bed is ideal but can be chewed.

advise a stone bowl, since learning my lesson the hard way. English Springer puppies like to carry bowls around in their mouths; this is alright with food bowls because they are usually empty before they pick them up. However, water bowls don't get emptied so fast, unless they are tipped all over the floor first, so if you put a stone one down it will be so much harder to pick up and carry.

There are also some excellent metal Spaniel feeding bowls and snoods on the

Your puppy will need food and water bowls and a supply of the food to which he has become accustomed.

market to ensure that their ears don't go in the food. This is important, because once you start allowing food to dry on the ears you are encouraging all sorts of unhygienic problems. In addition, the puppy may start chewing his own ears to remove the food and this could lead to other health problems.

BONES

You've probably heard this before, but it is so important: never give puppies (or adult dogs) bones that can splinter, and this most certainly includes chicken bones. The only safe bones, in my opinion, are marrow bones and the simulated bones. However, marrow bones do smell after a while, even if you cook them first. The simulated sterilized marrow bones obtainable from most pet shops are just as good as the real ones, but without the mess. More importantly, the dogs seem to like them. Bones can help to keep their teeth clean, and also provide some relief to puppies during their teething stage.

■ Collar, lead and identity disc

Puppies grow so fast that it's not worth buying an expensive collar and lead until they are about four to five months old. If you buy at this age, it is likely that the collar will expand and fit the puppy when he is older. Thus, any lightweight collar and lead will suffice until then.

The 'proper' collar should be made of rolled stitched leather and you will need a long, strong leather lead. I always recommend a rolled collar because the flat type tends to break all the hair around the neck area and make it coarse if a dog is wearing one all the time.

A lightweight identity disc must be on any collar from day one 'just in case' the pup accidentally escapes. The disc is also a legal requirement; any dog in a public place (including parks) must wear a collar and disc which bears the name, address and telephone number of the dog's owner.

Puppies love to chew, whether it's a marrow bone, a simulated bone or a toy.

■ **Toys**

Over the years I have given our puppies all sorts of toys, and have found that the ones that keep them amused the longest are 'kongs', tug toys and a piece of cotton rag about 1 m x 45 cm (3 ft x 18 in) with a double knot tied in the middle (this always gets disgustingly dirty and can either be washed or replaced). Any product made from 'nylabone', which can be chewed and chewed, is also very good. These are more expensive than most chews, but last for what seems like forever – even with an English Springer. I cannot abide squeaky toys because they either get quickly chewed to bits, or you get so fed up listening to the squeak that

Material tug toys and sturdy rubber 'kongs' make ideal toys for puppies and also for older Springers.

you wish it had been! There is also a danger with these toys: if the puppy does destroy it and swallow the squeak, surgery may be required to remove it.

COLLECTING YOUR PUPPY

When you go to collect your puppy you need to be prepared for the journey home. It is likely to be the first time he has been in a car and he may well be sick. Just in case this happens, take:

- Plenty of tissues
- Some old newspapers
- A carrier bag for the rubbish
- A towel will probably be handy in case the pup starts to dribble

I find that the easiest journey for a puppy is when someone is holding him on the back seat of the car, as this reduces the problem of him being thrown around. Cover the back seat and then put a towel across your knee in case of 'accidents'.

First thing in the morning is a good time to collect your puppy. Choose a day when you will have lots of time to settle him in and reassure him. It will be very frightening for the puppy going into your home – until now he will have felt safe and happy in his own environment and your home will feel strange at first.

Your puppy in his new home

- A puppy needs lots of sleep while he is growing. When you consider that an English Springer Spaniel will probably reach his full height at around six to nine months old, he has certainly got a lot of eating, sleeping and growing to do.

- The best thing to do when a new puppy arrives in your home is to feed him according to the breeder's diet sheet, encourage him to go to the toilet and put him in his bed for a sleep – he will probably be very tired with all the excitement of moving home.

Basic training

Basic training for your puppy should start within a couple of days (i.e. once he has settled into your home) and this should cover house-training, bathing and grooming. When the puppy is about twelve weeks old you can teach him some basic obedience, such as 'sit', 'stay' and walking on a lead (see page 66). It is worth remembering that all training is successful if you set aside sufficient time for it and remember to be very patient. Repeat your instructions clearly time and time again and acknowledge success with lots of praise and reward.

House-training

- Until your puppy arrived at your home, his toilet needs were satisfied by stopping and doing his business whenever and wherever he wanted to. When he was born, he would not have been able to move about for a few weeks and his mother would have kept the whelping box clean by eating the faeces. As soon as the puppy started to move about and his mother stopped cleaning up after him, he would have soon learnt to go outside his sleeping area when he wanted to go to the toilet – the puppy's alternative was to sleep in a dirty bed.

■ At this stage of a puppy's life, his whole world revolves around eating and sleeping. So it follows that he relieves himself each time he wakes and after each meal; the puppy has formed a habit. This habit is likely to continue as he goes through puppyhood, and you need to realise and tap into this if you are to house-train your puppy successfully.

■ Once he has slept or eaten, the puppy will need to relieve himself. It is likely that he will not go in his own dogbed but on your kitchen floor or lounge carpet, which has become the area outside his bed. The puppy knows no different as yet and should not be scolded for it.

THINGS TO TAKE HOME

A reputable breeder may give you the following when you collect your puppy:
■ Kennel Club registration documents (which you will need to complete to transfer the puppy into your name).
■ A feeding chart and a few days' supply of the food the puppy has been used to eating.
■ An Insurance Cover Note for the puppy.
■ A pedigree.
■ A receipt for the sale.
■ Details of any worming tablets that the puppy may have had.
■ Details of any vaccination programme that may have been started.
Note: reputable breeders will also tell you to contact them if you have a problem with your puppy; in other words, after sales service!

■ A new routine must be formed to replace existing toilet habits, and it is your responsibility to recognise the pup's needs and create a place for him to relieve himself. This requires quite a bit of effort on your part, but it is more than feasible to toilet train a puppy to newspaper in about seven to ten days. You must be prepared to act as soon as the pup either finishes eating or wakes from sleep. A puppy usually passes a motion after each meal, but will pass water frequently. It is worth remembering at this point that a young puppy cannot hold his water and has to go as soon as he gets that 'feeling'. It is only as a puppy grows older that he will develop the technique of being able to wait to go outside.

Training to newspaper

■ When we have a new puppy that needs house-training we use sheets of newspaper on the floor. Our puppy would have access to a living room and kitchen, so the floors of those rooms would be covered in newspaper several sheets thick. Each time the puppy has been fed or wakes up, we put him on the newspaper and try to keep him

there until he has relieved himself.

■ To begin with, you need a large area of newspaper to encourage the puppy to stay on it! Once he has relieved himself, we praise the puppy a lot, telling him how good he is in a positive tone of voice. We then remove the soiled paper and put fresh newspaper down.

■ As the puppy gets used to the idea, you will find that he will run to the newspaper to relieve himself – you should continue to praise him each time. At this point, I would like to share with you one of our house-training disasters. My husband used to have a habit of reading the evening newspaper whilst lying on the sitting room carpet, until one fateful day when our partially house-trained puppy ran over and wet all over that day's news – needless to say, we praised the puppy.

■ Put some newspaper down in each room so that the puppy doesn't have too far to travel in the early stages of his training. Over the next few days you can reduce the size of the newspaper (so you can see the colour of the flooring again!) and, once the puppy has learned to use the paper, you can remove the paper from the living room to leave only a papered area in the kitchen.

Training to go outside

■ Once the puppy is trained to the sheet of newspaper in the kitchen, his training

starts to change. When you are at home, you can leave the kitchen door open and place the paper outside the door so that the puppy can see it; encourage the puppy to go outside. Gradually you can eliminate the newspaper and the puppy will follow you outside to the area where you wish him to relieve himself.

■ Obviously, it is much easier for the owner to house-train a puppy if it's not cold weather! Over a period of time (with much love and praise for the puppy as he will always want to please you), you will find that, as long as the kitchen door is open, the puppy will go outside to relieve himself.

■ Most new owners I have spoken to seem to forget that a puppy will not necessarily be capable of being totally clean at night until he is around six to nine months old (even if he is going outside during the day). You may need to keep the newspapers down at night until the puppy can control his bladder. You can help by avoiding feeding him late at night and making sure that he always goes outside to relieve himself last thing before you go to bed.

■ One last tip: don't expect an English Springer puppy to go outside to relieve himself if you stay inside and shut the kitchen door behind him. My experience has been that he will be extremely 'upset', think that he is missing out on something because you are inside, and will sit by the door and wait for you. Then, when you let him back in thinking he has done his job, he will probably perform on your kitchen floor! While he is a puppy, I'm afraid that you are best going outside with him and waiting.

BATHING AND GROOMING YOUR PUPPY

Bathing

I like to get my puppies used to being bathed at an early age. Some pups really enjoy it, whereas others hate it at first. Start whilst your puppy is still young; it is much easier to hold onto a struggling pup than a struggling adult. We bathe our dogs in our full-size bath, sitting them on a bath mat so they don't slip, and using the shower hose to wash and rinse them.

Use a shampoo which has been specially prepared for a dog's coat; your vet will probably advise you as to which one. Sometimes human shampoos can cause skin irritations, so you should be careful with these. The principles of washing a dog are much like those of bathing a baby:

- Don't use very hot water
- Avoid getting soap in the eyes or inside the ears
- Don't let the dog slip in the bath
- Rinse the coat well until the water runs clear
- Use lots of towels to dry the dog

The puppy will probably want to shake himself, so use a large towel to cover the dog and thereby ensure that the wallpaper and paintwork stay dry and intact. In warm weather you can leave your puppy to dry naturally or use a hair dryer on a warm heat setting.

Grooming

At an early age the coat will still be baby hair and the only grooming you need to do is to brush and comb your puppy using a soft brush and a close-toothed spaniel comb. As with bathing, if you start young enough a puppy will soon learn to enjoy being groomed.

FEEDING YOUR PUPPY

I have included this section in the book because you may not be given a feeding chart with your puppy, or you may be unhappy with the one provided.

Over the years, I have tried and tested many types of dog food on my own dogs, and I am now a great believer in the quality complete foods which have been designed to provide all the nutrients a dog needs. These are both convenient and economical. They differ according to the age of the dog and you must always feed one specifically designed for a puppy (usually for the age range from three weeks to eighteen months). This will take into account the fact that he is still growing and has to build healthy bone and body tissue.

Feeding guidelines

■ You should speak to your vet and be guided by his advice regarding the choice of a suitable puppy food.

■ Do not feed poor-quality food to a growing puppy – you will most certainly encounter problems later on in his life.

■ A good-quality food will certainly contain protein, carbohydrates, vitamins and minerals in the required quantities. Protein contains all the necessary dietary needs for fitness and growth, whereas carbohydrates and fats will provide for a good supply of energy. Equally, vitamins and minerals are an essential part of all dogs' diets; the commonest minerals, calcium and phosphorus, are especially important for building and strengthening bones and teeth.

■ A good-quality complete food is an essential expense and is suitable for everyday feeding without the addition of any extras, apart from water.

■ The quantity of food that your puppy needs will vary as he grows, and he should be fed small amounts regularly and often, gradually increasing the amount according to his age.

■ Fresh water should be available to the puppy at all times.

■ Do not worry about feeding the puppy the same food all the time. Puppies are not like humans in wanting variety and, in any case, some puppies can react to changes in their diet with digestive upsets.

■ The amount that you feed your puppy each mealtime is an individual calculation, but you should be guided by the manufacturer's instructions. However, be careful as these are sometimes over-generous! As a guide, you should aim for a puppy that is well covered but still retains his shape (i.e. you can feel his ribs and see his waistline). The number of meals per day that you should feed a growing puppy is reproduced (right).

TRAINING AND MAINTENANCE

Note: there are other areas applicable to training and general maintenance which are relevant to a puppy and also to an adult dog. They are covered collectively in the next chapter.

How many meals?

■ Up to eighteen weeks old: four meals per day at regular intervals.

■ Up to nine months old: three meals per day at regular intervals.

■ Up to eighteen months old: two meals per day at regular intervals.

■ Over eighteen months old: only one meal per day is required.

Note: you may prefer to split this into two smaller meals and continue to feed the dog in the morning and early evening. I find with my dogs that doing this settles them better, but you must decide what is best for your dog and feed him accordingly.

WHEN IS A PUPPY NOT A PUPPY?

The answer is always different, according to the particular action being discussed. If we are talking about exercising, fun and games and logical thinking, then English Springers have discovered the secret of eternal youth – they think that they are always puppies and have never grown up. Where house-training is concerned, by about nine months the 'accidents' at night should have stopped; provided you have played your part in taking responsible action as discussed earlier (see page 45). Most English Springers will have reached their full height by about nine months, and will have fully matured in the body by the time they are two to three years old. Some males can take much longer.

CHAPTER FOUR

THE ADULT DOG

FOOD AND TREATS

This chapter links very closely with the previous one on the puppy, and takes your dog through adulthood and into his later years (in which he is usually termed a 'veteran'). There is information on feeding, preventative health care, grooming and bathing, socialization and training, exercise, car travel, visits to the vet, going on holiday and caring for the older dog.

Feeding your dog

We have already seen how important it is to feed a good-quality food to your English Springer in order to keep him looking good and in top-class condition. Here are some guidelines for feeding the adult dog.

■ Always make sure that fresh water is accessible to your dog at all times.

■ After your dog has finished eating, always take the feeding bowl away from him immediately. If your dog doesn't eat everything, offer it again a short while later. By leaving the bowl on the floor, not only are you encouraging house flies and other insects, but you are also training your dog to become a fussy eater, being

Adult English Springer Spaniels need plenty of exercise and you must be prepared to devote some time to this every day in all weathers.

allowed to wander back to the feeding bowl when he chooses. In all the years I have owned English Springers I have never had a fussy eater. I've found they eat rather fast and will devour most things!

Fussy eaters

People often say that they don't like feeding their dog the same food all the time, and he must get bored with it. With an English Springer I've never found this to be a problem. Many owners who claim that their dogs are fussy eaters often find that it is because they have been fed some really choice cuts. As a result, their dogs are now turning their noses up at ordinary food. They have become choosy because they know there is a possibility of something better on offer.

Treats

Many owners like to feed dog biscuits or treats in between main meals. In fact, some of the latest quality products on

FEEDING BOWLS

There are some excellent metal Spaniel feeding bowls and snoods on the market to ensure that their ears don't go in the food. This factor is important, because once you start allowing food to dry on the ears you are encouraging all sorts of unhygienic problems. Also your dog may start chewing his own ears to get the food off and this could lead to health problems.

the market can help to clean teeth and even exercise a dog's jaws. One thing to remember, however, is that most of these add extra calories to the daily diet and need to be included in the overall quantity of feed per day. Too many treats may result in an overweight dog. Dog treats are very useful when training your dog or rewarding good behaviour, but do feed those specifically for dogs and not for humans. Likewise, don't feed titbits from the table at meal times; this is a bad habit and one that English Springers learn very fast.

PREVENTATIVE HEALTH CARE

There are a number of preventative measures that you can take yourself to keep your dog healthy.

Cleaning ears

This is probably the most important preventative health care issue for an English Springer Spaniel and, if you do not clean the ears regularly, you will most certainly have long-term problems. Weekly cleaning with a special brand of gentle ear cleanser is required and this is obtainable through your vet. It is so simple to do but, as the ear is such a delicate area, it would be best if you ask your vet to show you how to do this properly – he will be only too pleased to give you advice. The hair around the inside of the ear canal should be regularly trimmed away to ensure that air can get inside the ear (see the notes on trimming, page 59).

Eyes

If a dog has a problem with his eyes, you will probably see him trying to rub at them with his paws. Dogs can suffer

WORMING

It is very important to worm your dog regularly. This is done by giving him a dose of tablets that is related to your dog's weight. The fact that you don't see any worms in the dog's faeces does not mean that your dog hasn't got any. I obtain the tablets from the vet and worm my dogs every four months. This simple task ensures that they stay worm free. If you are unsure about when to worm your Springer, you should ask your vet for advice.

Check your dog's eyes every day for discharge, tear stains or redness.

Your dog's teeth should look white and healthy if cleaned daily.

conjunctivitis just like humans do; they may also get something, such as a grass seed, in their eyes. Check your dog's eyes daily (it only takes a moment), and look for a discharge or tear stains from the corner of the eye; or a redness of the eyeball with the bottom rim of the eye socket looking loose and sore. If you find any evidence of these things, you should have your dog examined by a vet.

Cleaning teeth

A dog, like humans, has two sets of teeth. The first set of teeth starts to arrive when a puppy is about three weeks of age and should have come through by the time he is eight weeks old. However at about three months of age, these baby teeth will start

to loosen, and by the time a dog is about five months old, they will have been replaced by the adult teeth. Daily cleaning, from an early age, will usually ensure that your dog's teeth stay healthy and free from tartar; having your dog's

FLEAS

Fleas are very rarely seen on a dog but, again, that does not mean the dog is free of them. A sign of fleas is when you notice your dog scratching, possibly causing an area of his body to become red and inflamed. Your vet will be able to advise you of a suitable product to use to ensure that your dog is not troubled by fleas.

teeth scaled by a vet can be quite expensive as this usually involves an anaesthetic. You should buy toothpaste specially formulated for dogs (this doesn't need rinsing) and a finger-style toothbrush through your vet. Never use human toothpaste for your dog as this is not meant to be swallowed and could cause him to have gastritis.

Nails

Dogs' nails grow rather quickly and should be checked regularly to ensure they aren't too long. If your dog is exercised on concrete then the nails may wear down naturally, but, usually, English Springer owners have to resort to having their dogs' nails trimmed. This is especially important where a dog has dew claws as they will not wear down. As with everything, if you start early enough, your dog will let you trim his nails. I use a guillotine-type nail cutter, especially made for dogs, and, once you understand the make-up of a dog's nail, you will be able to do nail trimming with some confidence. Nails have nerve endings (quicks) and you need to know how to find out where these are. Ask your vet to show you how to do it. If this doesn't appeal to you, then ask your vet to do the nail cutting for you.

FIRST AID KITS

A basic first aid kit for your dog is essential, both in the home and as a travel pack to take with you when you are out exercising your dog. Listed below are a few items that would be useful if your dog has an injury and you need to apply immediate first aid treatment.

■ Two cotton bandages to provide padding for a wound and also to hold the dressing in place.

■ A few cotton swabs to place against the wound or to apply as a pressure pad to stop any bleeding.

■ Adhesive tape to hold the dressing in place – the type that sticks to itself and not to the dog.

■ Antiseptic wipes to clean the wound.

■ A spare lead in case your lead breaks or to make a muzzle – sometimes an injured dog can snap if he is frightened.

■ A pair of tweezers for removing thorns or other foreign bodies.

■ Scissors for cutting bandages, trimming hair from a wound or cutting brambles tangled in a coat.

■ A pair of disposable gloves.

■ A waste bag for rubbish.

■ 'Rescue Remedy' – this is a homeopathic recipe which is available from all good health shops and helps to treat shock in both humans and animals.

Important: whenever you have to administer any type of first aid to your dog, always ask a vet to examine the dog as soon as possible after the injury.

GROOMING

Adult English Springers have very beautiful, long, well-feathered ears and profuse silky hair on their chest, legs and underbelly. All this needs to be regularly groomed and kept clean and free from knots. When your puppy is about six months old his coat will start to become much thicker, and you will have to start trimming the excess hair so that he retains his natural shape and looks.

For a pet trim, the areas you will need to work on are around the inside of the ears, the top of the head and the top of the outside of the ear, the chest and throat, and the feet and hocks. If you are planning to show your dog, then you will

GROOMING EQUIPMENT

Although you can manage initially with just some basic grooming equipment, if you are going to cope with caring for you Springer's coat yourself, you will need the following equipment: small bristle brush, pin headed brush, wide and fine toothed comb, thinning scissors and pointed-end scissors, nail clippers, toothbrush and stripping comb.

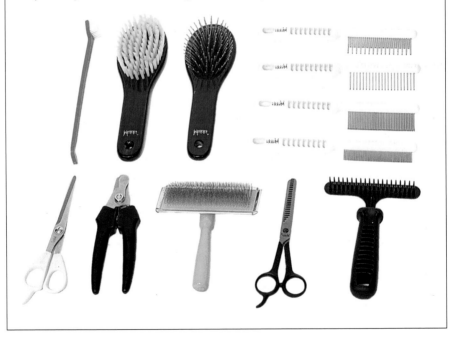

Use the comb and brushes to remove all dust, dirt, tangles and dead hair from the coat. The close-toothed spaniel comb and the slicker brush are particularly effective on the ear feathering. Don't be rough with your dog when you are grooming him; remember that there's real live skin under the hair!

have to learn to trim him in a more specialized manner, and you should get further advice on this from your nearest breed club Secretary.

You can learn to do a basic trim yourself or you can take your dog to a grooming parlour. However, a word of warning here: make sure the parlour knows how to trim an English Springer properly. Some groomers take the quick way out and run the clippers over the whole coat; this will definitely ruin it, and the soft silky hair will very likely grow back wavy and coarse. Always ask for your dog to be hand-trimmed.

Trimming your dog

If you do choose to learn to trim your own dog, the easiest way is to be shown in a practical demonstration. If you have bought your puppy from a reputable

breeder, they will probably be only too willing to show you. If this is not the case, once again, ask your nearest breed club Secretary to put you in touch with someone who will. For trimming at home you will need the following specialized grooming equipment:

- A pair of straight-edged scissors.
- A pair of thinning scissors.
- An ordinary-toothed steel comb.
- A close-toothed steel comb (known as a spaniel comb).
- A soft bristle brush.
- A hard bristle brush.
- A slicker brush (with 'L' shaped metal teeth).
- Two rubber thumbs (the kind cashiers use to count notes), or a rubber glove.
- A trimming table or bench with a non-slip rubber mat – it is much easier to groom a dog on a trimming table or

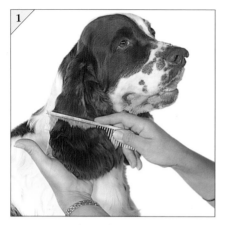

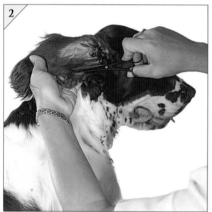

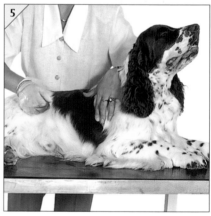

1 Use the spaniel comb and slicker brush on the ear feathering.
2 Carefully trim inside the ears with some thinning scissors.
3 Thin out the hair from the top of the ear to one-third down.
4 Pluck out any dead hair on top of the dog's head, wearing rubber gloves.
5 Use a brush to remove dust and dirt from the coat. Gently tease out any tangles and knots.

workbench rather than at floor level. The dog soon associates the table with the grooming routine.

■ Inside the ear around the entrance to the ear canal, the hair should be trimmed quite short to allow air to circulate freely into the ear. You should use the thinning scissors to do this. They can also be used to trim the hair on the outside of the ear flap. The hair from the top of the ear to about a third of the way down should be thinned out. After thinning, use the spaniel comb to remove all loose hair from the ear.

■ The hair on top of your dog's head is likely to go a lighter shade and stick up when it is dead hair and, therefore, needs to be trimmed out. All you need to do here is pluck out the dead hair, using your thumb and forefinger. This is where the rubber thumbs or glove are useful to give a better grip on the hair. You can use this action to remove any dead hair from other parts of the dog's coat.

■ The hair on the chest and throat will, at some stage, need thinning out and, once again, you can do this with the thinning scissors and a comb. As with

The long feathering of the coat needs to be combed regularly and kept free from knots.

Comb through the feathering on the chest carefully, teasing out any knots.

any aspect of trimming, always work against the natural lie of the hair.

■ The feet should be trimmed using a pair of straight-edge scissors; the aim is to make each foot look tight and rounded. This also means trimming flat any hair growing up between the toes, and any growing underneath the foot. The hair on the hocks should be trimmed close using the thinning scissors.

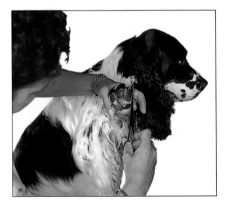

BATHING

Whether you are bathing a puppy or an adult dog, the process is the same (see page 49) but the calories used by the owner are far greater when bathing an adult English Springer!

The great debate on this subject is about how often you should bath your dog – I would recommend that you do it as often as you think your dog needs it. My dogs are regularly shown, and so I bath them frequently and have never experienced any adverse effects with their skin and coat condition. However, some people would disagree with this and believe that dogs should not be bathed unless absolutely necessary. I think that you should do whatever is best for your dog and your lifestyle.

Note: to ensure that your English Springer co-operates with you on the trimming table, remember to start your grooming routine early on in his life. While I use brushes and combs from an early age, I usually pretend to trim, using scissors at the same time, so that the puppy gets used to the noise they make. This practice pays off later on when I am using them for real. With patience on your part, your puppy will grow to love the routine and enjoy the attention.

Trim any hair growing between the toes and under the foot.

SOCIALIZING

Socializing is so important for your English Springer if you are to end up with a well-balanced dog that can mix successfully with other animals and humans in any situation. Let your puppy meet as many grown-ups and children as possible, but make sure you are there (especially where children are concerned) so the puppy does not come to any harm.

When your puppy's vaccinations are effective, you should try to take him to as many different places as you can, letting him experience as much as possible. It is interesting to note that puppy walkers for potential Guide Dogs for the Blind in the UK consider this to be one of the most essential parts of a youngster's training, and you should be thinking along these lines too.

In your home it is wise to let the puppy experience things such as noises from the television, radio, vacuum cleaner and washing machine, so that he quickly realises that these are part of everyday life. Finally, I am a great believer in leaving the radio on when I go out so that our dogs are not left in silence – I find this settles them down extremely well. English Springers are not fussy – they'll listen to any station!

EXERCISING

Try not to over-exercise your puppy, especially before he is six months of age. Young muscles and bones need time to develop fully and, as he is likely to reach almost full height by this age, all your puppy really should be doing is eating, sleeping and playing with short, controlled periods of exercise. An adult English Springer in peak condition will have unlimited energy so save the serious long-distance exercising for later when he is fully developed.

Exercise guidelines

■ You should always keep your dog on a lead until you are confident that he is under control, and always keep the lead on where there is heavy traffic or there are farm animals about.

■ Never allow your dog to chase anything – it is a habit that is very hard to break.

■ Respect other people's property and public areas; for example, keep your dog out of other people's private gardens and cultivated fields.

■ Remember to always carry some plastic bags in your pocket and pick up any dog faeces, placing them in a waste bin out of harm's way.

■ Take advice on what to do in the case of an accident happening to your dog in a place where veterinary attention is not immediately available, and always carry a basic first aid kit with you.

TRAINING YOUR DOG

A properly trained English Springer Spaniel is a constant source of pleasure and pride and, what's more, the training programme leading up to this should be fun for both you and your dog. Work hard, set high standards but, most of all, enjoy it. English Springers need to be motivated and will respond well to praise and rewards – a happy dog works harder because he wants to please.

I always find it fascinating to try to understand how a dog's brain operates, so for me this is the main point where training is concerned. Your English Springer does not think like you and me; he responds to circumstances or instinct. So it is far better to train your dog for reward (treat or praise) than to continually give negative commands and hope that he can work out what you really want. For example, if you were to allow your dog to continually sit on your knee as a puppy and you make a fuss of him at the same time, he would begin to associate this as a pleasurable experience.

REWARDING YOUR DOG

Praise your dog and be encouraging as soon as he shows even the slightest understanding. The timing of the praise is crucial; remember to praise at the time of the correct action, not before or after the event. Poor timing is the biggest cause of badly trained dogs.

However, one day, he will weigh about 22 kg (50 lb) and will still want to sit on your knee. Are you prepared for this? Your dog will not understand and will get confused if you suddenly start shouting that this is wrong. Actions like this will do nothing to build up a relationship of trust and understanding with your English Springer Spaniel.

The moral is clear: be precise and show your dog calmly and patiently what is required from the start. Use simple commands and stick to them. The tone of your voice is so important – it's not so much what you say as the way in which you say it.

BASIC TRAINING

Walking on a lead

■ I find that training a puppy to walk on a lead can be the most difficult. With a collar on, your puppy is no longer a 'free spirit' and sometimes rebels accordingly.

■ Use a soft collar at first (such as a cat collar) and get the puppy used to the idea of wearing it. Don't be surprised if he tries to get the collar off initially; be patient and he will soon forget that he is wearing one.

■ Later on, you can attach a lightweight lead to the collar and let your puppy get accustomed to it by walking around with the lead trailing on the floor. You need to be watching at all times in case he gets tangled up in the lead.

■ When your puppy is used to the idea of the extension to his collar, you can start to train him to walk with you attached to the other end of the lead! Lots of praise, encouragement and some dog treats will soon have him happily walking properly by your side. Remember to be consistent, and use the same words each time so that you don't confuse the command. Hand signals can also help your dog understand.

TRAINING TIP

You will need lots of patience as there are no short-cuts to training. The length of the training varies with each dog and, as with anything in life, you can only establish a routine by constant repetition.

■ Once your puppy is used to a collar and lead, you will need to start to develop control and you can do this by training him on a long lead (flexi leads are ideal for this). This will enable him to feel that he is free running, but will allow you to have full control at all times and will ensure that he responds immediately when called.

'Sit'

■ One of the first things you will probably want to teach your puppy is to sit on command. Stand in front of your Springer and get him to look up at you – a titbit in your hand usually does the trick. As your pup looks at you it will be natural for him to sit so that he can see you easily.

■ As soon as his bottom hits the ground and he is in the sitting position, say the command 'sit' and then his name. Praise your dog for achieving the command and reward him with a titbit.

■ With practice it won't be long before he learns this command. Don't forget that any training sessions should be short and fun. Always end on a positive note with lots of praise – that way your Springer will look forward to them.

'Stay'

■ The command 'stay' usually follows on from when you have taught your Springer to sit. When he sits on your command try encouraging him to hold the position by using the word 'stay', saying it firmly in a long drawn-out way (Staaay).

■ A visual signal to the dog is helpful here – hold your hand up encouraging him to hold the position.

BASIC TRAINING

- Do not move away from the dog and do not praise him until you wish him to break the stay.

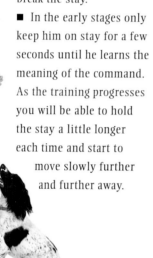

- In the early stages only keep him on stay for a few seconds until he learns the meaning of the command. As the training progresses you will be able to hold the stay a little longer each time and start to move slowly further and further away.

'Come'

- This is an important command to teach your dog before you let him off the lead! If you haven't taught him the command he'll have no idea what you are trying to do. When he does eventually return, you may be feeling quite exasperated and scold him. Never do this – after all, would you come back the next time if you knew you were going to be scolded?

- The secret is to start as early as you can, in the confines of your own home as soon as you get your puppy. Frequently call him to you throughout the day saying his name and the word 'come'. Use titbits and lots of love and attention to make sure he wants to come to you right away. He has to think of it as a pleasant experience.

- When you go out for the first time and let him off the lead you must continually call him back for titbits and praise. So a short walk and then call him back, another short walk and call him back and so on.

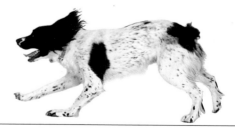

'Down'

■ As with teaching your dog to sit, you can use the same natural technique to teach him to lie down. Every time your dog lies down to rest, say the word 'down' and then his name.

■ Another natural method is to get down on the floor beside your dog and when you are at his level you can use a favourite titbit as an inducement to get him to lie down.

■ Put the titbit in your hand at floor level and encourage him to reach for it. Your dog will probably lie down to try and get it from you. The moment he lies down say the word 'down' and then his name, letting him have the titbit along with lots of praise. You've got to keep practising until it becomes second nature for your dog to obey as soon as you give the command.

VIDEOS AND CLASSES

A lot of specialist information is available today to show you how to train your dog. I am a great believer in visual training for the trainer, and recommend that you invest in one of the many basic obedience training videos. Such is the importance of a well trained dog that satellite television now includes some good programmes.

Training classes are also a good idea and can help with the socialization of your puppy. Look for a quality training class rather than the one that is closest to where you live, and make sure that the instructors are properly qualified. You should visit the class before you enrol and expect to see friendly faces and happy dogs, not lots of shouting and the overuse of choke chains.

CAR TRAVEL

Many dogs, unused to travelling, suffer from motion sickness – some because they are nervous about the experience and others because there is too much excitement. To get your dog accustomed to travelling in the car you should start him off at an early age with some short trips, making them into fun expeditions. Initially, the rolling motion of the car may make him sick, and the puppy should sit on someone's lap until he is used to the car's movement.

Later, when the dog is much more confident, it is important for your safety (and his) that he is restrained behind a dog guard, in a dog travel harness or in a purpose-built car cage.

English Springers can be restrained safely in a purpose-built cage in the back of the car. This will help prevent injuries in the event of an accident.

A special heat-reflective blanket may be used in hot weather, but the car door must be left open.

WARNING

Finally, never leave your dog locked in a car on a hot day – even with the windows open. A car is like an oven and the temperature can increase rapidly, in which case your dog could soon collapse and would be likely to die.

VISITS TO THE VET

I must admit that I've never had any problems visiting the vet. I decided to speak to my own vet, however, to get some ideas about the problems that you could experience.

■ The biggest problem seems to be with dogs that do not like being handled, and it is extremely difficult for a vet to examine a dog which is permanently struggling and frightened. It will help if you train your dog, from an early age, to stand or sit still while you (or anyone else who is around) gently run your hands all over him. This should include looking at his teeth and inside his ears, and examining his paws. If you regularly groom your dog, and clean his teeth and ears, visits to the vet should not cause any problems.

■ You might also like to practise giving your dog medication and bathing his eyes. This is something most people don't do until their dog is ill, and they then have great difficulty in administering the

essential medication. Ask your vet to show you how to do this so that you can practise it from puppyhood.

■ Another problem seems to be the owner's attitude towards the annual 'booster', i.e. the yearly renewal of the vaccinations. The booster injection is a vaccine which protects against many potentially fatal illnesses. However, most vets don't just give a booster – included in the price is an annual health check for your dog and, hopefully, a reassurance that all is well. If only life was as simple for us!

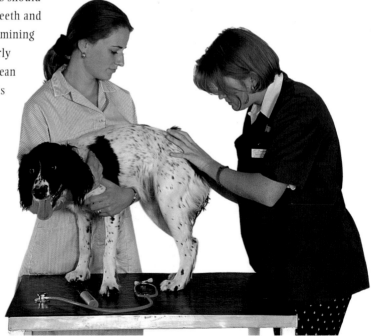

GOING ON HOLIDAY

The first thing to consider is whether to take your dog on holiday with you. Some people wouldn't dream of going away without their dog, and choose holidays that allow him to go everywhere with them. I find this very restricting, especially where children are concerned. I prefer to leave the dogs at home with a very responsible person to look after them full-time, or at a good-quality boarding kennel. However, there are some things to be aware of if you do intend to use a boarding kennel.

■ Ask around to see if people are willing to recommend a boarding kennel to you – and check it out before you book in the dog.

■ Make sure you book well in advance – there should be no last-minute panic. The kennel staff will usually need confirmation of boarding dates and the expected time of arrival and collection.

■ Take along any current vaccination certificates, as most kennels will not accept dogs without these. Also have a word with your vet about an extra vaccination against kennel cough.

■ Make sure your dog is wearing his collar and identity tag. You should also take an old blanket or toy with you, as something with a familiar scent will help to reassure and settle your dog. Let the kennel staff know what you call your dog so they can talk to him each day.

■ It is very helpful for the kennels, in the event of an emergency, to have the name and telephone number of someone who could be contacted in your absence, e.g. a friend or a family member.

■ You could also give them the name and telephone number of your vet. Details of any medical conditions should be carefully explained, and instructions about medication are best given to the kennel staff in writing. This is also applicable to any special dietary needs.

VETERANS

In the show world a veteran is a dog of seven years and over. From this age onwards, you may find that your dog needs extra care and attention with regard to feeding. Some older dogs can have problems with their digestive systems. If you feed a quality complete food, you will probably find that there is one in the range formulated especially for older dogs which will prevent digestive problems.

Another problem to guard against with older dogs whose exercise is restricted, is the length of their nails which may become too long and affect the dog's ability to walk.

As with any pet, the day will inevitably arrive when your English Springer Spaniel no longer has a quality of life and you will have to make that very painful decision – be guided by your vet and acknowledge that whatever happens it is in the best interest of your dog. As I write this, I can feel the tears for every dog I've lost – believe me, it doesn't get any easier over the years – but part of the pleasure of owning an English Springer Spaniel comes from the responsibility involved and from knowing that your dog is waiting at home and relying on you to feed and care for him right to the end.

Every English Springer Spaniel owner has a duty to their dog and should endeavour to establish a caring and responsible routine on which their dog can always rely. It is only by doing this that your English Springer will form a natural and permanent bond with you – something this breed does extremely well, their unconditional love being quite astounding.

CHAPTER FIVE

BREEDING

THE FIRST STEPS

Most English Springer Spaniel breeders breed dogs purely as a hobby and combine it with showing or working their dogs. Their overall aim is to produce the best possible specimen of an English Springer Spaniel, which breeds true to type without weakness or deterioration; either physical or mental. By type, I mean English Springers that belong to the same family lines and which are so alike in general appearance that they can be recognised without difficulty. These dogs usually represent the results of a definite breeding plan, carried through several generations.

The average pet owner who breeds English Springers does so initially by accident. Some are dog lovers who have acquired a puppy, first and foremost as a pet, but they decide to get involved in breeding because their English Springer Spaniel has done rather well in the show ring, and this fuels their ambition to

acquire another one. However, to produce a good specimen you have to start off with quality stock of quality lines.

To breed or not to breed?

As the owner of an English Springer Spaniel puppy, think long and hard before you decide to get involved with breeding. If you would like another English Springer, it may be much better for you to purchase one from a reputable breeder. If you want a dog that is related to your original English Springer, go back to its breeder and buy one from the same lines.

Questions to ask yourself

Answer the questions in the box on page 76 to see if you are prepared to breed from your Springer. Don't mate your bitch if you have answered 'No' to any of these questions. The answer to all these questions should be 'Yes' if you are to proceed with the mating.

Mating

You should seek advice from your veterinary surgeon and an experienced dog breeder before embarking on breeding a litter. It may also be a good idea to read a specialist book on breeding.

It is important that the bitch is mated at the right time if she is to conceive, and in maiden bitches it is preferable to use an experienced and proven dog. A bitch is usually receptive towards a dog's advances

NOTES ON MISMATING

If your bitch is ever mismated (i.e. mated unintentionally) it is very important to act immediately to avoid an unwanted pregnancy. An injection to avert pregnancy can only be given within forty-eight hours of mating. Therefore, it is advisable to visit your veterinary surgeon at once if mismating occurs.

between the tenth and the thirteenth days of her season. However, each bitch is an individual and each season may be different.

You should always ask the stud dog owner whether they will let you use their dog, and give them plenty of warning of the likely date. Never take it as a forgone conclusion that they will agree to your bitch being mated by their dog because you are paying a stud fee. Some stud dog owners only let their dogs mate bitches of a certain line. You will almost certainly be asked to take your bitch to the stud dog, and will be required to pay the stud fee at the time of mating. It is important to be guided by the owner of the experienced stud dog; they will know what is best for both the dog and the bitch.

If you are new to all of this, you should be aware of a couple of things that are likely to happen during the mating. Firstly, if she doesn't like the idea of the dog mating her, your normally placid and

QUESTIONS TO ASK BEFORE YOU BREED FROM YOUR SPRINGER

- Is your bitch Kennel Club registered and in your name?
- Is your bitch in good health?
- Is your bitch's vaccination and worming up to date?
- Does she have a good temperament?
- Will she be under eight years old when she whelps the pups? The Kennel Club won't let you register the litter if she isn't. The ideal time for a first litter is thought to be about eighteen months old, and certainly no later than five years.
- Is she from good-quality stock?
- Is she free from all hereditary defects?
- Has she been tested clear under all the necessary health schemes? You should take advice from your nearest Breed Club for details of how to get her tested.
- Have you chosen a suitable stud dog, and given it the same consideration as your bitch regarding hereditary defects and health schemes?
- Have you chosen a stud dog that is proven?
- Will you be able to afford the stud fee?
- Are you prepared to look after your bitch properly throughout her pregnancy?
- Are you prepared to be there with her for the whelping?
- Are you prepared for any expensive vet's bills which may be incurred for health checks during the pregnancy, and for the whelping?
- Are you prepared to help the bitch nurse her puppies if she can't feed them?
- Have you got somewhere suitable for the bitch to have her puppies?
- Are you prepared to wean the puppies, i.e. teach them how to lap/eat on their own?
- Do you have somewhere clean, safe, airy, dry and warm where the pups can sleep and play without coming to any harm when they can move around?
- Are you prepared to feed, clean and handle the pups after they have been weaned, until they are ready to go to permanent homes?
- Do you realise that once a pup starts to walk, he can move about quite a lot and cover a large area? From three weeks onwards, you will be responsible for feeding him. He will need five meals per day until he is eight weeks old. Pups go to the toilet after each meal and make a lot of puddles in between. Multiply all of that by eight puppies and you've got your hands full!
- Are you prepared to socialize the pups so that they grow up well balanced?
- Are you prepared for what can be a full-time job of puppy rearing?
- Are you prepared to vet all potential owners to make sure that your puppies go to the most suitable homes?
- Are you prepared to look after your puppies until they are all sold? They may not all go at eight weeks old.
- Are you prepared to be responsible for stock which you have bred? If the owner no longer wants the dog you may be asked to take it back.

friendly bitch may turn into 'the hound from hell', snapping and growling out of character. It may be necessary to put a muzzle on her so that no-one gets hurt during the mating.

Secondly, the muscles in the bitch's vagina contract at the end of penetration, preventing the stud dog's penis from being withdrawn. This constitutes the 'tie' that is a desirable feature of mating, and which mostly, but not always, occurs. The dog, still attached to the bitch, will step over her (or be turned by the handlers into this position) so the animals are back to back and 'fixed' in position. There is no point trying to separate dogs which are locked in this way, since the dog can only be released when the bitch is ready (the old wives tale of buckets of cold water only ever results in wet dogs!). It is important for both dogs to be held steady during this process so that neither of them gets hurt. The time of a tie varies greatly, usually from about ten to forty minutes, but I have been told of some lasting much longer.

Once the tie is complete and the dogs separate, you will be able to take your bitch home. A drink of glucose in water seems to settle the bitch down for the journey home. You should ask the stud dog's owner to sign a Kennel Club application for litter registration by the breeder to prove that their dog mated your bitch, and on what date. This form should be obtained from the Kennel Club in advance of the mating and will be completed by you when registering your puppies.

NOTE

If your bitch does not conceive, most reputable stud dog owners will offer you a free service mating for your bitch on her next season. This should be established when you make the initial inquiry with the stud dog owner.

PREGNANCY AND WHELPING

Pregnancy usually lasts about sixty-three days from the date of mating, but may be anywhere between fifty-seven and sixty-nine days. From the date of mating, I always change the bitch's food to one specially made for bitches in whelp; this ensures that extra vitamins and minerals are given throughout the whole pregnancy. During the last three weeks of pregnancy our bitches are fed about one-third more food than normal divided into several small meals throughout the day. Some people say that bitches may go off their food but I have never found this to be the case.

Your bitch should be checked by the vet throughout her pregnancy. Take her to the vet about four weeks after mating to check if she is in whelp (don't wait until the last minute to find out if there are any pups). This is a relatively simple procedure and the vet may use an ultra scan; the same equipment as used to see human babies. Although it cannot identify how many pups there are, it can confirm that they exist, and allow you to make the necessary arrangements.

One of the things I do when the bitch is about seven to eight weeks in whelp, is to make sure that the bitch is trimmed properly, as it will be a while after the pups are born before she will want to keep still for trimming. I also bath her and make sure that her nipples and surrounding areas of skin are scrupulously clean, to aid feeding her pups. At about the same time, I introduce her to the whelping box and try to persuade her to sleep in it from then onwards.

It's a good idea to ask the vet to check the bitch every day from her sixty-third day of pregnancy onwards. The lives of the bitch and her puppies are precious, and you need to be sure that all is proceeding well.

Whelping day

It can be normal for a bitch to refuse food for up to twenty-four hours when whelping is imminent. Another sign is her temperature dropping from normal which can be between 38.3-38.7°C (100.9-101.7°F) to about 36.6°C (98°F). Ask your vet to show you how to take your dog's temperature. The actual labour is in two stages.

■ **Stage I** of labour may last from about two to twenty-four hours. During this stage the bitch will be restless and will pant compulsively. The whelping box should be in a quiet secluded place and lined with lots of newspaper. It is normal behaviour for the bitch to shred this paper during the early stages. I would never let a bitch go longer than twenty-four hours in this stage without having her checked out by a vet.

■ **Stage II** of labour begins with the first big expelling contraction, or straining movement, and it is important to make a note of when this occurs. If the first puppy has not appeared after an hour the vet should be contacted. It could be that a puppy is stuck (possibly too big to come out naturally) and you may need veterinary assistance to remove it. Failure to act quickly could result in the litter being lost, and you would also be putting your bitch's life in danger.

■ Normally a dark coloured sac of fluid (the water bag) will appear at the vulva, ahead of the first puppy. Again, you will need to note the time in case of problems later. Be careful, because the water bag may burst outside the whelping box, possibly when the bitch is trying to relieve herself. The puppy, wrapped in a fluid-filled sac, should be born very soon after the water bag. The

---

WHELPING BOX

You will need a strong whelping box about 90 x 120 cm (3 x 4 ft) in size. There should be a whelping rail on all sides to stop the pups being squashed by their mother. The rail should be 12.5 cm (5 in) up from the floor and 10 cm (4 in) from the sides.

---

bitch should tear open this sac at once to release the puppy and will proceed to lick it dry. If she cannot do this, it will have to be done for her. Hold the puppy in a piece of dry towelling and carefully tear open the sac using your fingers. Gently rub the puppy dry using the towel, and hold it upside down to drain any fluid from its lungs.

■ The pup's umbilical cord is attached to the placenta (afterbirth) which should soon be expelled by the bitch. This is a piece of liver-like tissue, which the bitch will usually eat while attempting to clear up the fluids that have escaped during the birth of the puppy. Green and brown

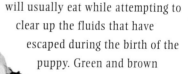

79

staining from these fluids is normal. The bitch usually severs the pup's umbilical cord from the afterbirth. If she doesn't know what to do, and the puppy remains attached to it, you will have to break the cord with your fingers, or cut it with a sterilized pair of scissors. This should be done 2.5-5 cm (1-2 in) from the pup's stomach, being extremely careful not to pull on the stomach wall. Use clean hands and make sure that you wash them afterwards. The puppy should be checked for any abnormalities, such as a cleft palate (i.e. no roof to its mouth). Your vet should be contacted right away if you find any malformed puppies.

- If the bitch is not ready to give birth to another one right away, she may settle down and try to feed the puppy. You may need to give some help by gently opening its mouth and placing it on a nipple. Hold the pup there until it starts suckling. If your bitch is ready to give birth again, she will not want to feed the puppy. However, it is also likely that she will not want to let the puppy out of her sight. I put some warm towels in a small cardboard box, then lay the pup in this in

These seven-week old puppies are still in the 'nest' before leaving their mother and litter-mates to go to new homes.

DOCKING

If you wish the puppies' tails to be docked, or to have the dew claws removed, this will need to be done by the time they are four days old. English Springers are, by nature, merry and active animals who love to explore through heavy vegetation (and, unfortunately for the pet owner, brambles). The fast wagging action of an undocked tail can easily lead to it being torn and bleeding. This is extremely painful for the dog and very difficult to treat and heal fully.

Until 1993 in the UK, tail docking was carried out either by experienced breeders or veterinary surgeons. From the 1st July 1993 the British Government amended the Veterinary Surgeons Act to say that it was only lawful for a vet to dock tails. However, around the same time, the Royal College of Veterinary Surgeons ruled that docking by vets was unethical, unless for therapeutic or acceptable protective or preventative reasons. As a result, a lot of vets will not now dock tails. There is an organisation called the Council of Docked Breeds, consisting of breeders, owners and supporters of docked breeds, and also some vets. It has been set up specifically to fight against the 'ban on docking' law.

If you are intending to breed a litter of English Springer Spaniels and would like your puppies' tails to be docked, it is in your own interest to gather information well before the bitch is mated. First of all, ask your own vet if they dock and, if the answer is no, contact the Council of Docked Breeds for information regarding suitable vets who do. Also, if your own bitch is docked, you could speak to her breeder for advice and guidance.

I have been breeding English Springer Spaniels for over twenty years and have always had my pups' tails docked. I have found it to be a perfectly humane process, but you must decide when you have a litter, what is best for your pups, and, of course, your conscience.

a corner of the whelping box. The bitch can see where the pup is and will usually be content to get on with giving birth. The cardboard box will also ensure that the pup doesn't get stood on by the bitch. Some warm milk with some glucose added will be very welcome to the mother at this stage. If there is a delay of more than two hours between births, when it is obvious that there are more pups to come, you should contact your vet for advice.

■ It is wise to keep a note of the number of afterbirths passed; there should be one for each puppy. A retained afterbirth can be dangerous – contact your vet immediately after whelping if you think they have not all been expelled.

■ It is always advisable to ask your vet to call at your home within twenty-four hours of whelping, to check the bitch and her puppies. If there are any puppies which have congenital abnormalities,

are comfortable, and gives the pups something to grip as they scramble around. Until you wean the pups at three weeks old, you will need to feed your bitch extra rations to ensure she has a good flow of milk.

Looking after your bitch and her puppies

Puppies cannot see or hear until they are about ten to fourteen days old, and a good bitch will look after her babies, keeping them clean and fed, and generally being there for them. She will continue in this dedicated role up until the time they are due for weaning. From the moment the pups are born, I like to leave a radio on low wherever the bitch is, so that she is not in total silence. In fact, I make sure that this practice is continued until the pups are ready to go at eight weeks, as I find it contributes towards their socializing.

Your vet should be called if you have any worries about the bitch or her puppies; don't trust to luck – puppies fade fast. Don't let all and sundry handle the puppies at this stage; your bitch may become protective if she feels in danger, and you are also exposing the pups to infection.

Weaning the puppies

■ I start weaning my pups at three weeks old, and have found the easiest way to do this is to start with a well-known brand of canned puppy food. A

such as a cleft palate, they will probably have to be put down.

■ Once the bitch has settled down with her litter it may be difficult to get her to leave the whelping box to go to the toilet. You may have to gently, but forcibly, remove her. In the interest of the pups' health, do not exercise your bitch outside the home environment while she is looking after them.

■ The floor of the whelping box should have a good supply of newspapers and be kept scrupulously clean. I put a large piece of vetbed on top of the newspapers. This ensures that the bitch and her pups

little of this food, mashed up with some warm water, will soon have them lapping. You should start the pups off by putting a little food in their mouths with your finger. The meaty smell nearly always encourages them to start eating straight away. After a few days, change their diet to a quality complete food for puppies on which the bitch has been fed. The food should be well soaked for the puppies and of a very soft, mushy consistency.

■ At three weeks old the pups' first teeth start to arrive and things begin to get a little uncomfortable for their mother! Make sure you trim the puppies' nails if they get too long, as they may rip

---

TIP

The six-week stage is a good point for you to worm the pups and the bitch for a second time. The puppies' nails may also need to be clipped again.

---

the skin around the bitch's nipples. This is also a good age to worm your pups for the first time. Obtain the worming tablets from your vet and be guided by their instructions. The bitch should also be done at this stage.

The mother will continue to feed the pups for about five to six weeks.

HOMING YOUR PUPPIES

Eight weeks old and it's time for the pups to go to their new homes. Hopefully, you will have excellent homes for all your puppies, and will have vetted the potential buyers. As a responsible breeder you should give the new owners:

■ The Kennel Club registration documents (which they will need to complete to transfer the pup into their name).

■ A Pedigree.

■ A feeding chart and a few days' supply of the food the pup has been used to eating.

■ A receipt for the sale.

■ Details of any worming tablets the pup may have had.

■ Details of any vaccination programme you may have started.

You will probably want to tell the new owners to contact you if they have a problem with their puppy. I also give the new owner an Insurance Cover Note which insures the pup for about six weeks following the sale. The Kennel Club offer this type of service when you register your puppies with them. Your vet will also have details of independent insurance companies offering the same service.

Very often when a puppy is leaving to go to a new home, their new owner will say to me, 'How can you bear to let the pups go?' My answer is always the same: if I kept all the puppies, they would have to share my love and attention, and when this is divided up they would only receive a small portion of it. By going to a new home, with new owners, who have been extremely well vetted, I know that they will get 100 per cent of the love and attention, 100 per cent of the time. This helps me to let them go with a happy(ish) heart, although I do have to keep a box of tissues at the ready!

■ The bitch will feed the pups until they are five to six weeks old, although somewhat sporadically as time goes on. This is alright, as her milk is excellent for them. However, when you feed the pups, choose a time when their mother has been away from them for a while so you can be sure that they are hungry.

■ From three to eight weeks old you should feed the puppies five meals a day. These meals should increase in size as the pups get bigger. I usually alternate between feeding dry and soaked food at each meal.

■ Make sure that there is always fresh water available for the pups. I always let their mother clean the bowl after the pups have been fed; that way she doesn't feel left out. Finally, you may find that the bitch starts to regurgitate her food for the puppies. This is nothing to worry about – it's her way of weaning them.

■ By the time the pups are six weeks old they should be completely self sufficient in their feeding. Mentally, however, they are not ready to go into their new homes until they are eight weeks old.

CHAPTER SIX

SHOWING

DOG SHOWS

At some time you may find that you want to know more about dog shows and actually showing your own English Springer Spaniel. Perhaps you have visions of winning the Best in Show award at Crufts, but whether you have aspirations in this direction, or just want to know more about showing and generally having some fun, you may find that this chapter will provide you with the kind of information you need.

What is a dog show?

Dog shows, in one form or another, have been around for a very long time, their format changing over the period to provide for the needs of each era's exhibitors. We now see dog shows that run all the year round and are very well organised, providing a hobby that can be followed by all the members of the family. The shows come in all shapes and sizes from single breed shows to full scale events. These may stand alone or be part of another event, such as a large agricultural show.

There are some criteria that your dog has to satisfy in order to be eligible for entry at one of the many thousands of shows and competitions licensed by the Kennel Club throughout the U.K.

■ Your English Springer has to be at least six months old on the first day of any dog show to be eligible for entry.

■ With the exception of Exemption Shows (see page 87), your dog also has to be officially registered at the Kennel Club. The breeder of your puppy has to register him initially, but it is your responsibility to transfer him into your ownership before you enter any shows.

SHOW LICENCES

Every Society recognised by the Kennel Club, wishing to run a dog show, has to obtain a licence from them. The Show Committee of that Society is then responsible for putting on a well organised show in accordance with Kennel Club rules. Part of their responsibility is to provide a show schedule for potential exhibitors. These schedules are free of charge and provide all the information you need to make an entry.

Entry forms

All exhibitors have to sign an entry form each time they enter a show whereby they agree to abide by Kennel Club rules when exhibiting. Completed entry forms are sent to the Show Secretary with the correct entry fee, by the official closing date. Late entries are not accepted. By signing the entry form the exhibitor declares that the dog(s) entered will not be exhibited if they contract (or are in contact with) any infectious diseases within the six-week period prior to the show. Also that the dog(s) will be correctly prepared for exhibition and the exhibitor will abide by Kennel Club rules and regulations.

Once the entry form has been accepted by the Show Secretary, then a contract is formed between the exhibitor and the Society. It is important to read the Schedule before entering. Most Show Secretaries are only too pleased to give advice to new exhibitors.

The competition

The competition you will be up against at a dog show will depend on the type of show you enter. Basically, there are four types of competition that you are likely to encounter:

■ Only English Springer Spaniels
■ Other breeds of spaniels from within the Gundog group
■ All other breeds from the Gundog group
■ All other breeds in the six groups (i.e. Gundogs, Hounds, Terriers, Toys, Utility and Working breeds). Each of these can be split into dogs only, bitches only, or mixed sex classes.

The description of the types of shows you may enter doesn't stop here. Taking into account each of these categories, there are different types of shows geared to accommodating dogs at different levels of winning – a sort of handicapping system.

Within each show there are classes you can enter and these are usually based on the sex of your English Springer, and/or its age, and/or the amount he has previously won.

Types of Dog Shows

■ Exemption Shows

The name 'exemption' is given because the show is exempt from the Kennel Club rules regarding the running of dog

OBTAINING SHOW SCHEDULES

Shows are advertised in various doggy publications but the main source of information is found in the canine press. In the U.K., there are two weekly dog newspapers which include all the advertisements for future shows. All you have to do is contact the Show Secretary and ask to be sent you a show schedule. The newspapers also include a critique on the winners of each show, written by the actual show judges.

shows. All other types of shows require entries to be sent to the Show Secretary in advance, but you are allowed to enter this one on the day. Dogs that have not been registered with the Kennel Club can also be entered at this type of show, i.e. both pedigree and non-pedigree dogs.

The show is for all breeds and consists of four classes for pedigrees only, and about six to eight novelty classes for both pedigree and non-pedigree dogs.

Exemption shows are very useful for giving new puppies (and new handlers) some valuable experience. Entry fees are low and they are, therefore, an inexpensive way for novices and experienced showgoers, young and old,

to have some fun and support a good cause at the same time.

■ **Primary Shows**

These are fairly new types of shows which are quite small in the size of their classification and you can only enter if you are a member of the Society running them. In most instances, you can easily become a member by paying a nominal membership fee at the show. You can enter on the day but dogs do have to be Kennel Club registered. Dogs that have previously won prizes counting towards becoming a Champion, or a first prize in anything other than a puppy class, cannot be entered at this type of show. Entry fees at Primary Shows are low.

■ **Sanction and Limited Shows**

These two types of shows are very similar in that entries must be made about two to four weeks before the date of the show and only members of the Society can enter. Once again, membership fees can be paid with your entries. Sanction and Limited Shows are generally for all breeds or linked to a particular group – in your case the Gundog group will be relevant. Entry fees are extremely reasonable.

■ **Open Shows**

These shows are very popular and can be single breed shows, Spaniels only, Gundogs only or all breeds. Entries are more expensive than at the other shows mentioned, but still within the means of

WHY SHOW AT ALL?

Dog shows are very much like any other exhibitor-based show. You are putting forward your dog to be judged against other dogs, to find out whether the judge considers him to be the best example present. Every dog exhibited should be assessed by the judge against its respective breed standard. Show judges are usually highly respected breeders and exhibitors, who have achieved good standards with their own dogs and whose opinion is generally sought after.

The English Springer Spaniel Breed Standard can be found on page 14, and you may like to consult this to see how your dog measures up before you decide whether or not to show him. This is not as easy as it sounds, and it might be worth taking some advice and guidance from the breeder of your English Springer, or from your nearest Breed Club Secretary.

Types of English Springer

There are two different types of English Springer Spaniel: the 'Working' type and the 'Show' type. At this point, I think it only fair to mention that whilst you can enter both types at a dog show, the 'Working' type of Springer does not do as well in the awards as the 'Show' type does.

most exhibitors. This type of show is open to all dogs and exhibitors – hence the name 'Open Show'. This means you can enter your dog regardless of what he has won before. Entries are usually made about three to four weeks in advance.

■ **Championship Shows**

This is where the serious top-level showing takes place – where it is possible for your dog to win an award towards becoming a Champion. Entries to the show are usually made about eight weeks in advance of the show date and are quite expensive, sometimes costing up to four or five times more than an Open Show entry fee. However, entry fees at a Breed Club Championship Show are much more reasonable.

Many Championship Shows take place out of doors during the summer months, and they can be a single breed show, a Gundog show or an all breed one. Whatever the type of Championship Show, you will generally compete against English Springer Spaniels of the same sex, unless you choose to enter some of the special stakes classes also. Breed classes work on a type of knock-out system and the winners of each class, if remaining unbeaten, can compete for the ultimate award in either Dogs or Bitches. This is a Challenge Certificate, also known as a CC.

If you win three of these CCs, under three different Judges (with at least one of the CCs being awarded when the dog was more than twelve months old), your English Springer Spaniel will be a Show Champion.

TRAINING FOR THE SHOWRING

One of the most important things you need to do is to train your puppy from an early age with some of the necessities required for him to be judged in the showring.

Standing

A judge will need your puppy to stand in a show pose in order to properly assess him against the Breed Standard. This position is displayed on page 88 and allows the dog's outline to be shown off. The handler holds the dog by placing one hand on the muzzle while using the other hand to hold up the tail. All dogs, whatever their age, have to stand in this position to be judged, but it is especially difficult to get a puppy to stand still for the required amount of time. Most judges (including myself) will make allowances for young high-spirited pups who get fed up having to stand still.

It is best to start training your dog to do this at an early age. I start standing the puppy at six to eight weeks for about 30 seconds or so, just so he gets an idea of what's required. This time should be built up slowly, incorporating looking at the pup's teeth and running your hands all over his body. This is easier to do if you have someone helping you and it is very important to get your pup used to

it, as a judge will need to do this to make an assessment. Be careful not to overdo this when the puppy is teething as he may be upset about having his mouth looked at and could be ruined for later on in the showring.

Moving

A judge will ask you to move your dog in order to assess his movement. This involves either moving 'straight up and down' or in 'a triangle'.

- **Straight up and down** means moving away from the judge in a straight line so that your dog's rear movement can be assessed, and also coming back towards them in the same straight line

---

SHOW TRAINING CLASSES

Contact the Secretary of your local general Canine Society (you can get this information from the Kennel Club) to find out about your nearest weekly show training class. You can take your puppy along as soon as he has had all his vaccinations and the vet confirms it's all right for him to mix with other dogs. Show training classes are usually run by experienced exhibitors, and will enable your pup to socialize with other puppies and adult dogs in controlled circumstances; this really is a valuable source of training.

for the front movement to be assessed. Sometimes the judge will move to the side to assess the dog's movement. If this happens, make sure you do not put yourself between your dog and the judge. This is a very common error when moving a dog and spoils the judge's view.

■ **A triangle** involves moving your dog in a triangle to allow the rear, side and front movement to be easily assessed by the judge. This is much easier for the judge to assess a dog, but unfortunately the showring in which you are exhibiting doesn't always allow the luxury of triangular movement. Once again, when you are moving, do not put yourself between your dog and the judge.

The dog should be moved at a steady pace; this is generally likened to a brisk walk but it can be different speeds for individual dogs and you should take advice on this. Your dog should be trained to move wearing a lightweight show lead which usually has a collar built into it in the same material. If possible, the dog should be taught to move along with his head up and showing himself off. Some dogs are naturals at this, but I'm afraid I am still waiting to find one – my dogs usually need a lot of hard work to get them to this stage, as they always seem to want to put their heads down and sniff the ground!

As with standing, training a puppy to move properly in the showring can also start at an early age. However, I recommend

---

SHOW ETIQUETTE

With regards to etiquette at a dog show, there are a few important things you might want to remember:
■ Do not talk to the judge in the ring unless you are asked a question.
■ Do not allow your dog to interfere with other dogs in the ring.
■ Do not leave the ring until the ring steward or judge tells you it is all right to do so.
■ Remember that the judge is in charge of the ring at all times and his decision is final. If you would like to know what the judge thought of your dog, it is permitted to ask, but not while the Judging is taking place. You must wait until after he has finished judging for the day.
■ Remember to keep accurate records of shows entered and your results so you can keep track when making further entries.

---

that you never take your dog for a proper walk on a show lead. Only use it to practise standing and movement for competitions. You'll be surprised how quickly the puppy learns the difference between going for a walk and moving for a show.

Your first show

Sorry to disappoint you but, in my opinion, your first show should be without the dog! Just go along to watch what goes on in each ring and what's expected of each exhibitor. Choose a local show, to make this as painless as possible.

It's all right reading about it, but I really think you need to experience some of the practical side before you take a dog with you. And don't forget that you can't take a dog to a show if it isn't entered, so leave it at home on this occasion.

Pre-show preparation

So your puppy has been trained and the show entry sent off in good time. Bathing and trimming has been done according to the guidance set out in earlier chapters. Your show bag has been packed with things you might need: some grooming equipment for that last-minute preparation, a bowl and some dog food and water (and maybe something for the exhibitors too). The show lead also needs to be packed, together with a blanket or piece of Vetbed for your dog to lie on while you're both waiting for your turn. At some of the larger outdoor shows it is also advisable to take

something for you to sit on. Most of the Championship Shows are benched shows and this means your dog will have to be kept on a wooden bench-type cubicle while he is waiting to be shown. In this case, you will also need a strong benching chain and a leather collar so your dog remains secure. However, I wouldn't recommend leaving an inexperienced dog alone on a bench in case he becomes distressed and injures himself.

Show Secretaries sometimes send entry passes in advance of the show and you will need to check your schedule to see if you should have received them. You will need a pin to fasten your exhibitor's identification number (your number will be given to you at the show), and don't forget it's fastened to you not the dog!

At the show

■ The first thing to do when you arrive at the show is to buy a catalogue. This will give you details of all dogs entered at the show. It will also give the names and addresses of all the exhibitors. You may find someone living near you with the same hobby!

■ Check that your entry is included and that it contains the right details. If you find anything wrong, tell the Show Secretary immediately and they will advise you what will happen next. Invariably you will still be showing your dog, but the nature of the mistake may involve you being transferred to another class, or corresponding with the Kennel Club after the event. This may mean the possibility of any awards being disqualified. As discussed earlier, it is important for you to get the information right on the entry form.

■ The second thing to do is find out which ring you will be showing your dog in, and at what time. Some shows have a lot of rings and it is your responsibility to be in the right place at the right time. If you miss your class, you cannot be transferred to another one.

■ When it's time for you and your dog to go into the ring, follow the instructions of the ring steward. The judge has overall control of the ring but it is the ring steward's responsibility to assist him in the course of his duties, and to ensure the smooth and efficient running of the showring at all times.

■ Hopefully, you will be familiar with ring procedure. Before you actually go into the ring for your turn, it may also be possible to watch the procedure adopted by your judge regarding the examination and movement of the dogs. The first class your dog goes into under a particular judge will mean that it will need to be fully examined and moved. If you are entered in another class under the same judge, on the same day, they will probably not examine or move your dog again and will remember the details when judging the class. The ring steward will tell you where to stand in the ring when this is going to happen.

■ On completion of the judging of any class the judge will place the winners in descending order, from left to right, in the centre of the ring. Prize cards are usually given for first, second, third, Reserve (fourth) and sometimes there is also an award for VHC (Very Highly Commended, or fifth).

SUMMARY

So all your training and show preparation will have paid off, and even if you don't win, valuable experience will have been gained and you'll live to show again! Over the years, you will hopefully find success and enjoyment from your hobby and, remember, no matter what happens, if you love your English Springer Spaniel, you will always be taking the best dog home.

PART THREE

HEALTHCARE

In this section on healthcare, there is expert practical advice on how to keep your dog fit and healthy and prevent many common health problems, together with information on canine illnesses and infectious diseases and the special health problems that may affect the English Springer Spaniel as a breed, especially inherited ones. If you are considering breeding from your English Springer, you will find everything that you need to know about genetically inherited diseases. Essential first-aid techniques for use in a wide range of common accidents and emergencies, including road accidents and dog fights, are also featured, with easy-to-follow step-by-step illustrated guides, and advice on simple first aid measures that you can do yourself and when you should seek expert veterinary help.

7

HEALTH MAINTENANCE

Throughout the health section of this book, where comments relate equally to the dog or the bitch, we have used the term 'he' to avoid the repeated, clumsy use of 'he or she'.

SIGNS OF A HEALTHY DOG

■ **Appearance and behaviour**
In general, a healthy dog looks healthy. He wants to play with you, as games are a very important part of a dog's life. A Springer, being developed as a working gun dog, should always be ready for his walk, and will require a lot of exercise.

■ **Eyes and nose**
His eyes are bright and alert, and, apart from the small amount of 'sleep' in the inner corners, there is no discharge. His nose is usually cold and wet with no discharge, although a little clear fluid can be normal.

■ **Ears**
His ears are very sharp and responsive to sounds around him. The Springer Spaniel's ears, although not so exaggerated as a Cockers', are long and pendulous, very hairy, and hang down over the ear canal and side of the head. The inside of his ear flap is pale pink in appearance and silky in texture. No wax will be visible and there will be no unpleasant smell. He will not scratch his ears much, or shake his head excessively.

■ **Coat**
A healthy Springer Spaniel's coat will be glossy and feel pleasant to the touch. He will

not scratch excessively and scurf will be not be present. His coat will smell 'doggy' but not unpleasant, and he will probably continuously shed hairs (moult) to some degree, especially if he lives indoors with the family.

His tail, if docked, will be about one-quarter of the full length, although the working Springer is left with a longer tail than a show dog. The skin over the dock should be of normal thickness and should not irritate him. Many Springer Spaniels are now left undocked, in which case the tail will taper gradually to the tip and will be well feathered.

■ **Teeth**
The teeth of a healthy dog should be white and smooth. If they are yellow and dull there may be plaque or tartar formation.

■ **Claws**
The claws should not be broken or too long. There is a short non-sensitive tip, as in our nails. The claw should end at the ground, level with the pad. Dogs will not pay much attention to their feet, apart from normal washing, but excessive licking can indicate disease. Springers are born with five toes on the front feet, with one in our 'thumb' position called the dew claw, and usually four on the hind feet. Dew claws, especially on hind feet, are usually removed at three to five days of age as they become pendulous and are often injured as an adult.

■ **Stools**
Like all dogs, a healthy English Springer Spaniel will pass stools between once and six

POINTS OF THE ENGLISH SPRINGER SPANIEL

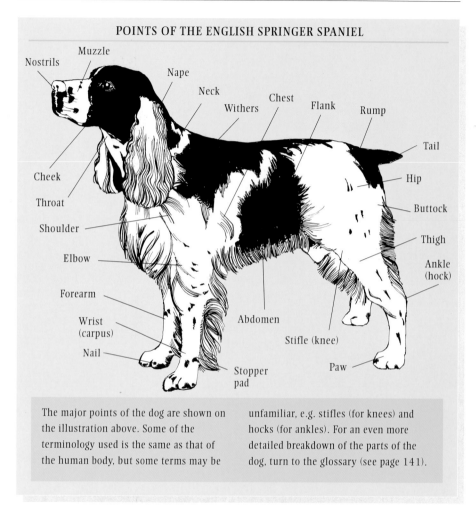

The major points of the dog are shown on the illustration above. Some of the terminology used is the same as that of the human body, but some terms may be unfamiliar, e.g. stifles (for knees) and hocks (for ankles). For an even more detailed breakdown of the parts of the dog, turn to the glossary (see page 141).

times a day depending on his diet, temperament, breed and opportunity.

■ **Urination**

A male will urinate numerous times on a walk as this is territorial behaviour. Bitches usually urinate less often.

■ **Weight**

A healthy Springer will look in good bodily condition – not too fat and not too thin. Sixty per cent of dogs nowadays are overweight, so balance the diet with the right amount of exercise.

■ **Feeding**

A healthy Springer will usually be ready for his meal and, once adult, he should be fed regularly at the same time each day. Most dogs require one meal a day, but some seem to require two meals daily just to maintain a normal weight. These are the very active dogs who tend to 'burn off' more calories.

EXAMINING YOUR DOG

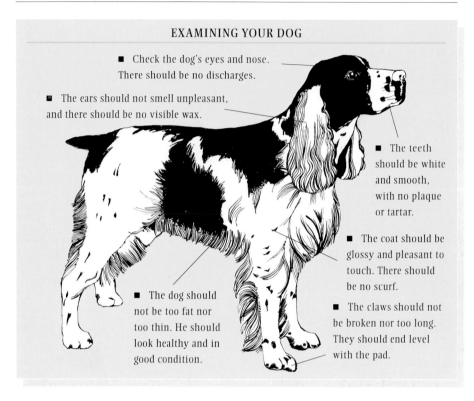

■ Check the dog's eyes and nose. There should be no discharges.

■ The ears should not smell unpleasant, and there should be no visible wax.

■ The teeth should be white and smooth, with no plaque or tartar.

■ The coat should be glossy and pleasant to touch. There should be no scurf.

■ The dog should not be too fat nor too thin. He should look healthy and in good condition.

■ The claws should not be broken nor too long. They should end level with the pad.

DIET

■ Feeding a puppy

The correct diet as a pup is essential to allow him to achieve his full potential during the growing phase. In a Springer Spaniel this is from fifteen to twenty months of age. Many home-made diets are deficient in various ingredients just because owners do not fully appreciate the balance that is required. It is far better to rely on one of the correctly formulated and prepared commercial diets which will contain the correct amounts and proportions of essential nutrients, such as protein, carbohydrates, fats, roughage, minerals, such as calcium and phosphorus, and essential vitamins.

Modern thinking is that the complete, dried, extruded diets available now have so many advantages that the new puppy could be put on to a 'growth' formula diet of this type from as early as four weeks. Crunchy diets such as these have advantages in dental care also.

However, there are some excellent canned and semi-moist diets available but care should be taken to check whether these are complete diets, or complementary foods which require biscuits and other ingredients to be added. If you really know your diets, it is of course possible to formulate a home-prepared diet from fresh ingredients. A puppy should be fed four times a day until he is three months of age, and with a complete dried food this can be left down so that he can help himself to food

CARE OF THE OLDER DOG

Provided that he has been well cared for throughout his life, there may be no need to treat the older Springer Spaniel any differently as old age approaches.

■ **Diet**

This should be chosen to:

■ Improve existing problems

■ Slow or prevent the development of disease

■ Enable the dog to maintain his ideal body weight

■ Be highly palatable and digestible

■ Contain an increased amount of fatty acids, vitamins (especially A, B and E) and certain minerals, notably zinc

■ Contain reduced amounts of protein, phosphorus and sodium

■ **Fitness and exercise**

A healthy Springer Spaniel should hardly need to reduce his exercise until he is over ten years old. There should be no sudden change in routine; a sudden increase in exercise is as wrong as a sudden drop. Let the dog tell you when he has had enough. If he lags behind, has difficulty in walking, breathing, or getting to his feet after a long walk, then it is time to consider a health check. As dogs age, they need a good diet, company, comfort, and a change of scenery to add interest to their lives.

■ **Avoiding obesity**

■ As the body ages, all body systems age with it. The heart and circulation, lungs, muscles and joints are not as efficient. These should all be able to support and transport a dog of the correct weight but they may fail

if the dog is grossly overweight.

■ A Springer Spaniel of normal weight will approach old age with a greater likelihood of reaching it. It is wise to diet your dog at this stage if you have let his weight increase. Food intake can be increased almost to normal when the weight loss has been achieved.

■ Reduce the calorie intake to about sixty per cent of normal, to encourage the conversion of body fat back into energy. Feed a high-fibre diet so that the dog does not feel hungry. Maintenance levels of essential nutrients, such as protein, vitamins and minerals, must be provided so that deficiencies do not occur.

■ Alternatively, your veterinary surgeon will be able to supply or advise on the choice of several prescription low-calorie diets, available in both dried and canned form, or instruct you on how to mix your own.

The dog's lifespan

Most people assume that seven years of our lives are equivalent to one year of a dog's. However, a more accurate comparison would be as follows:

■ 1 dog year = 15 human years

■ 3 dog years = 30 human years

■ 6 dog years = 40 human years

■ 9 dog years = 55 human years

■ 12 dog years = 65 human years

■ 15 dog years = 80 human years

Note: this is only an approximate guide as the larger breeds of dog tend not to live as long as the smaller breeds.

whenever he feels hungry. The exact amount of food will depend on his age and the type of food, and if instructions are not included on the packet, you should consult your vet.

At three months of age, he should be fed three times daily, but each meal should have more in it. By six months of age, he could be down to two larger meals a day, still of a puppy or growth formula food. He should remain on this type of food until twelve to eighteen months of age, and then change to an adult maintenance version.

■ **Feeding an adult dog**
Adult dogs can be fed on any one of the excellent range of quality dog foods now available. Your vet is the best person to advise you as to the best diet for your Springer, and this advice will vary depending on his age, amount of exercise and condition.

■ **Feeding an older dog**
From the age of ten to twelve years onwards, your Springer Spaniel may benefit from a change to a diet specially formulated for the older dog, as he will have differing requirements as his body organs age a little. Your vet is the best person to discuss this with, as he will be able to assess his general condition and requirements.

EXERCISE

Exercising a puppy

As a puppy, your Springer Spaniel should not be given too much exercise. At the age that you acquire him, usually six to eight weeks of age, he will need gentle, frequent forays into your garden, or other people's gardens provided they are not open to stray dogs. He can and should meet other vaccinated, reliable dogs or puppies and play with them. He will also enjoy energetic games with you, but

VACCINATIONS

Vaccination is the administration of a modified live, or killed, form of an infection which does not cause illness in the dog, but instead stimulates the formation of antibodies against the disease itself.

■ **Five major diseases**
There are five major diseases against which all dogs should be vaccinated. These are:
■ Canine distemper (also called hardpad)
■ Infectious canine hepatitis
■ Leptospirosis
■ Canine parvovirus
■ Kennel cough
Many vaccination courses now include a component against parainfluenza virus, one of the causes of kennel cough, that scourge of boarding and breeding kennels. A separate vaccine against bordetella, another cause of kennel cough, can be given in droplet form down the nose prior to your dog entering boarding kennels.

Note: all these diseases are described in Chapter Eight (see page 108).

■ **When to vaccinate**
In the puppy, vaccination should start at eight to ten weeks of age, and consists of a course of two injections, which are administered two to four weeks apart. It is recommended that adult dogs have an annual check-up and booster inoculation by the vet.

remember that in any tug-of-war type contest
you should win!

■ **Exercise and vaccinations**

Although you should be taking your puppy
out with you to accustom him to the sights
and sounds of normal life, at this stage you
should not put him down on the ground in
public places until the vaccination course is
completed, because of the risk of infection.

■ **Exercise after vaccinations**

About a week after his second vaccination, you
will be able to take him out for walks, but
remember that at this stage he is equivalent
to a toddler. His bones have not calcified,
his joints are still developing, and too
much strenuous exercise can affect normal
development. Perhaps three walks daily for
about half an hour each is ample by about four
months of age, rising to two to three hours by
the time he reaches six months. At this stage,
as his bones and joints develop, he could then
be taken for more vigorous runs in the country.
However, he should not be involved in really
tiring exercise until nine months to a year old,
by which time his joints have almost fully
matured, and his bones fully calcified.

Exercising an adult dog

■ **Exercise after six months**

As an adult dog, his exercise tolerance will be
almost limitless, certainly better than most of
ours! It is essential that such a lively, active,
intelligent breed as the Springer Spaniel has
an adequate amount of exercise daily – it is
not really sufficient to provide exercise just at
weekends. A daily quota of one to two hours
of interesting, energetic exercise is essential.

During exercise they enjoy games such as
retrieving and finding hidden objects, so try to
exercise his brain as well as his body.

DAILY CARE

There are several things that you should be
carrying out daily for your dog to keep him
in first-class condition.

■ **Grooming**

All dogs benefit from a daily grooming
session. Use a stiff brush or comb obtained
from your vet or pet shop, and ensure you
specify that it is for a Springer Spaniel as
brushes vary. Comb or brush in the direction
of the lie of the hair. Hair is constantly
growing and being shed, especially in dogs
that live indoors with us, as their bodies
become confused as to which season it is in
a uniformly warm house. Brushing removes
dead hair and scurf, and stimulates the
sebaceous glands to produce the natural oils
that keep the coat glossy.

■ **Bathing**

Dogs should not require frequent baths, but
can benefit from a periodic shampoo using a
dog shampoo with a conditioner included.

■ **Feeding**

Dogs do not benefit from a frequently changed

GENERAL INSPECTION

A full inspection of your dog is not
necessary on a daily basis, unless you
notice something different about him.
However, it is as well to cast your eyes
over him to ensure that:
■ The coat and skin are in good order
■ The eyes are bright
■ The ears are clean
■ The dog is not lame
Check that he has eaten his food, and
that his stools and urine look normal.

diet. Their digestive systems get used to a regular diet; dogs do not worry if they have the same every day (that is a human trait) so establish a complete nutritious diet that your dog enjoys and stick to it.

The day's food should be given at a regular time each day. Usually the adult dog will have one meal a day, at either breakfast-time or tea-time. Both are equally acceptable but ideally hard exercise should not be given within an hour of a full meal. Rather give a long walk and then feed on your return. Some dogs seem to like two smaller meals a day, and this is perfectly acceptable, provided that the total amount of food given is not excessive.

■ **Water**

Your Springer should have a full bowl of clean, fresh water changed once or twice a day, and this should be permanently available. This is particularly important if he is on a complete dried food.

■ **Toileting**

Your Springer should be let out into the garden first thing in the morning to toilet, and this can be taught quite easily on command and in a specified area of the garden. You should not take the dog out for a walk to toilet, unless you just do not have the space at home. The mess should be in your premises and then picked up and flushed down the toilet daily. Other people, children in particular, should not have to put up with our dogs' mess.

Throughout the day he should have access to a toileting area every few hours, and always last thing at night before you all turn in.

Dogs will usually want to, and can be conditioned to, defaecate immediately after a meal, so this should be encouraged.

■ **Company**

Springers are sociable dogs and bond to you strongly. There is no point having one unless

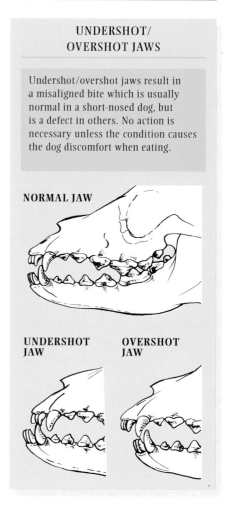

UNDERSHOT/ OVERSHOT JAWS

Undershot/overshot jaws result in a misaligned bite which is usually normal in a short-nosed dog, but is a defect in others. No action is necessary unless the condition causes the dog discomfort when eating.

NORMAL JAW

UNDERSHOT JAW

OVERSHOT JAW

you intend to be there most of the time. Obviously a well-trained and socialized adult should be capable of being left for one to three hours at a time, but puppies need constant attention if they are to grow up well balanced. Games, as mentioned before, are an essential daily pastime.

■ **Exercise**

Being bred originally as a gundog, your Springer will need a lot of exercise, so this breed is not

TEETH AND JAWS

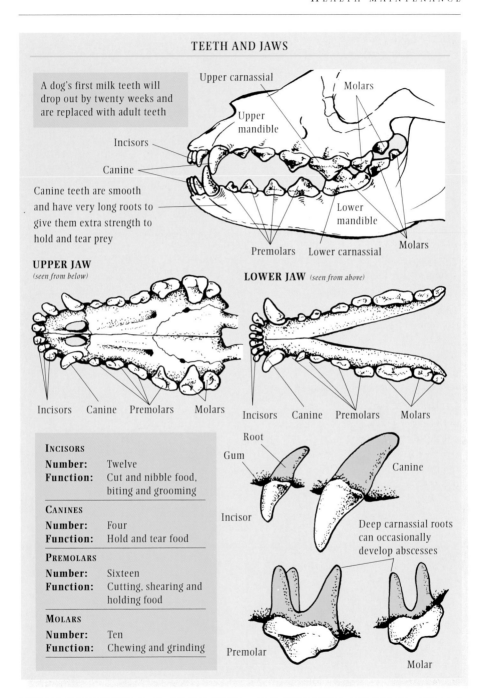

A dog's first milk teeth will drop out by twenty weeks and are replaced with adult teeth

Canine teeth are smooth and have very long roots to give them extra strength to hold and tear prey

Upper carnassial

Molars

Upper mandible

Incisors

Canine

Lower mandible

Premolars   Lower carnassial   Molars

UPPER JAW
(seen from below)

LOWER JAW *(seen from above)*

Incisors   Canine   Premolars   Molars

Incisors   Canine   Premolars   Molars

INCISORS	
Number:	Twelve
Function:	Cut and nibble food, biting and grooming

CANINES	
Number:	Four
Function:	Hold and tear food

PREMOLARS	
Number:	Sixteen
Function:	Cutting, shearing and holding food

MOLARS	
Number:	Ten
Function:	Chewing and grinding

Root

Gum

Canine

Incisor

Deep carnassial roots can occasionally develop abscesses

Premolar

Molar

one to choose if you want a quiet house dog. In addition, they are intelligent and need to have their brain exercised as well by varied interesting walks, games or by being worked.

- **Dental care**

Some complete diets are very crunchy. These by mimicking the diet of a wild dog, e.g. a fox or a wolf, which will eat a whole rabbit (bones, fur etc.) will help to keep your dog's teeth relatively free of plaque and tartar. However, a daily teeth inspection is sensible. Lift the lips and look at not just the front incisor and canine teeth but also the back premolars and molars. They should be a healthy, shiny white like ours.

If not, or if on a soft, canned or fresh meat diet, daily brushing using a toothbrush and enzyme toothpaste is advisable. Hide chew sticks help clean teeth, as do root vegetables, such as carrots, and many vets recommend a large raw marrow bone. These can, however, occasionally cause teeth to break. Various manufacturers have brought out tasty, chewy food items that can benefit teeth, and your vet

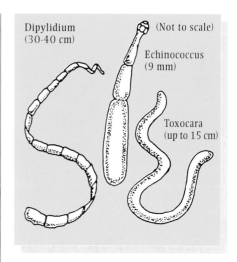

Dipylidium (30-40 cm)

Echinococcus (9 mm)

Toxocara (up to 15 cm)

(Not to scale)

WORMING YOUR DOG

Dogs need to be wormed regularly for roundworms:
- Fortnightly for puppies from two weeks to three months of age
- Monthly for puppies from three months to six months of age
- Twice yearly thereafter in male dogs and neutered females

Note: Bitches used for breeding have special requirements – ask your vet. Adult dogs should be wormed twice a year for tapeworms.

will be able to recommend a suitable one.

Pups are born with, or acquire shortly after birth, a full set of temporary teeth. These start to be shed at about sixteen weeks of age with the central incisors, and the transition from temporary to permanent teeth should be complete by six months of age. If extra teeth seem to be present, or if teeth seem out of position at this age, it is wise to see your vet.

PERIODIC HEALTHCARE

Worming

- **Roundworms (Toxocara)**

All puppies should be wormed fortnightly from two weeks to three months of age, then monthly up to six months of age. Thereafter in a male or neutered female Springer, you should worm only twice yearly. Dogs used for breeding have special roundworming requirements and you should consult your vet about these. There is evidence that females undergoing false (pseudo) pregnancies have roundworm larvae migrating in their tissues,

THE LIFE CYCLE OF THE DOG ROUNDWORM (TOXOCARA)

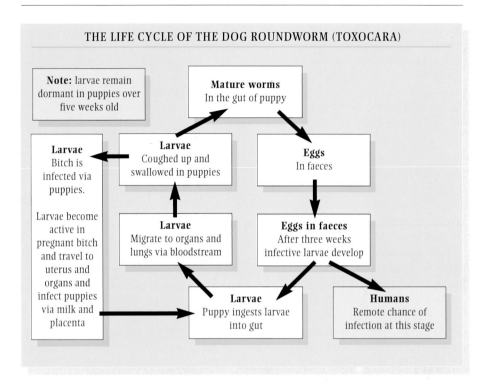

Note: larvae remain dormant in puppies over five weeks old

Mature worms
In the gut of puppy

Larvae
Bitch is infected via puppies.

Larvae become active in pregnant bitch and travel to uterus and organs and infect puppies via milk and placenta

Larvae
Coughed up and swallowed in puppies

Eggs
In faeces

Larvae
Migrate to organs and lungs via bloodstream

Eggs in faeces
After three weeks infective larvae develop

Larvae
Puppy ingests larvae into gut

Humans
Remote chance of infection at this stage

so they should be wormed at this time.

■ **Tapeworms (Dipylidium and Echinococcus)**

These need intermediate hosts (fleas and usually sheep offal respectively) to complete their life cycle, so prevention of contact with these is advisable. As a precaution, most vets recommend tapeworming adult dogs twice a year. There are very effective, safe combined round and tape wormers available now from your vet.

SPECIAL HEALTH PROBLEMS

The Springer Spaniel is usually a fit, friendly and interesting companion. There are, however, some health problems that are known to occur in this breed particularly. A few of the commoner problems are detailed below.

■ **Central Progressive Retinal Atrophy (CPRA)**

This is an inherited progressive degeneration of the retina of the eye which may lead to total blindness. There are two types of PRA – generalized and central – both types being seen in the English Springer Spaniel. PRA usually develops in the young adult. There is no treatment for PRA and the disease must be controlled by the testing of breeding dogs. Affected dogs must not be used for breeding.

■ **Retinal dysplasia**

This is a congenital defect which leads to the development of multiple folds in the retina. The effect on sight varies from no apparent effect to total blindness. It is inherited in the English Springer Spaniel.

■ **Glaucoma**

This is an inherited disease in Springers, and develops when the pressure of the fluid inside the eye increases, causing pain, inflammation, and excessive tear production.

■ **Entropion**

This is an inherited disease, usually of the young, growing dog, seen quite often in the Springer. The edge of an eyelid rolls in so that the lashes rub against the surface of the eye, causing irritation of the eyeball. The eye is sore and wet with tears, and often kept closed. Surgical treatment is necessary.

■ **Canine fucidosis**

This is a rare but severe, progressive and ultimately fatal disease that affects young adults. It is characterized by nervous signs such as in co-ordination, ataxia, loss of learned behaviour, deafness and visual impairment, and depression, which progress over a period of several months. It is inherited in the English Springer Spaniel and has been seen in the UK and in Australia. There is no treatment, but blood tests carried out at Cambridge University Veterinary School can identify carriers which should not be bred from.

■ **Hip dysplasia**

This is an inherited disease of the English Springer Spaniel and is dealt with more fully in Chapter Eight. It is a malformation of one or both hip joints, and may not be detectable until the dog is a young adult or even older. Stiffness on rising, an odd bunny-hopping gait, or lameness are the usual signs. Reduce the chances of your dog being affected by checking the hip scores of the puppy's parents, and by keeping exercise to a gentle level until your dog is at least six months old.

■ **Achalasia**

This is caused by a thickening of the cardiac sphincter which is the muscle at the entrance to the stomach from the oesophagus. The oesophagus cannot empty into the stomach fully, and gradually enlarges causing ballooning. Regurgitation of food occurs, and affected dogs have to be fed from a raised feeding bowl to prevent this. It is seen in the English Springer more often than many breeds.

■ **von Willebrand's disease**

This is an inherited disease of another blood component, the platelets, and causes haemorrhage. The Springer Spaniel is one of the breeds in which it is known to be inherited.

Important: in addition to the specific advice given above, reduce the chances of your new dog having these problems by asking the right questions about his ancestry before you purchase him. Apart from retinal dysplasia, PRA, and hip dysplasia, all the above problems are uncommon.

PET HEALTH INSURANCE AND VETS' FEES

By choosing wisely to start with, and then ensuring that your dog is fit, the right weight, occupied both mentally and physically, protected against disease by vaccination, and fed correctly, you should minimize any vets' bills. The unexpected may well happen though. Accidents and injuries occur, and dogs can develop lifelong allergies or long-term illnesses, such as diabetes. Pet health insurance is available and is recommended by most veterinarians for such unexpected eventualities. It is important to take out a policy that will suit you and your Springer Spaniel, so ask your veterinary surgeon for his recommendation.

CHAPTER EIGHT

DISEASES AND ILLNESSES

RESPIRATORY DISEASES

■ Rhinitis

This is an infection of the nose caused by viruses, bacteria or fungi. It occurs but is not very common in the Springer Spaniel. It may also be part of a disease, such as distemper or kennel cough. Sneezing or a clear or coloured discharge are the usual signs. Another cause, due to the dog's habit of sniffing, is a grass seed or other foreign object inhaled through the nostrils. The dog starts to sneeze violently, often after a walk through long grass.

■ Tumours of the nose

These are also occasionally seen in the English Springer Spaniel. The first sign is often haemorrhage from one nostril. X-rays reveal a mass in the nasal chamber.

Diseases producing a cough

A cough is a reflex which clears foreign matter from the bronchi, trachea and larynx. Severe inflammation of these structures will also stimulate the cough reflex.

■ Laryngitis, tracheitis and bronchitis

Inflammation of these structures can be

THE RESPIRATORY SYSTEM

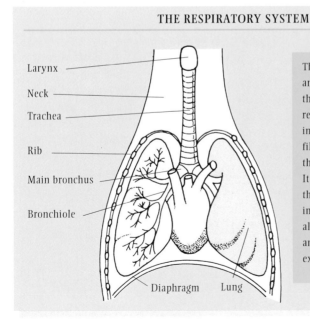

Larynx

Neck

Trachea

Rib

Main bronchus

Bronchiole

Diaphragm   Lung

The larynx, trachea, lungs and bronchi, together with the nose, make up the dog's respiratory system. Air is inhaled through the nose, filtered and passed through the larynx into the trachea. It enters the lungs through the bronchi, which subdivide into bronchioles and end in alveoli, or air sacs. Oxygen and carbon dioxide gases are exchanged in the alveoli.

INFECTIOUS DISEASES

- **Distemper (hardpad)**

This is a frequently fatal virus disease which usually affects dogs under one year of age. Affected dogs cough and have a discharge from the eyes and nose. Pneumonia often develops, and vomiting and diarrhoea usually follows. If the dog lives, nervous symptoms, such as fits, paralysis, or chorea (a type of regular twitch), are likely. The pads of the feet become thickened and hard – hence other name hardpad.

- **Treatment** by antibiotics may help, but the only real answer is prevention by vaccination as a puppy, and annual boosters.

- **Infectious canine hepatitis**

This affects the liver. In severe cases, the first sign may be a dog completely off his food, very depressed and collapsed. Some die suddenly. Recovery is unlikely from this severe form of the disease. Prevention by vaccination is essential.

- **Leptospirosis**

Two separate diseases affect dogs. Both, in addition to causing severe and often fatal disease in the dog, are infectious to humans. **Leptospira icterohaemorrhagiae** causes an acute infection of the liver, often leading to jaundice.
Leptospira canicola causes acute kidney disease.

- **Treatment** of both is often unsuccessful, and prevention by vaccination is essential.

- **Canine parvovirus**

This affects the bowels causing a sudden onset of vomiting and diarrhoea, often with blood, and severe depression. As death is usually due to dehydration, prompt replacement of the fluid and electrolyte loss is essential. In addition, antibiotics are also usually given to prevent secondary bacterial infection. Prevention by vaccination is essential.

- **Kennel cough**

This is a highly infectious cough occurs mainly in kennelled dogs. There are two main causes:
- Bordetella, a bacterial infection
- Parainfluenza virus

Both of these affect the trachea and lungs. Occasionally, a purulent discharge from the nose and eyes may develop. Antibiotics and rest are usually prescribed by the vet. Prevention of both by vaccination is highly recommended.

caused by infection, such as kennel cough or canine distemper, by irritant fumes or by foreign material. Usually, all three parts of the airway are affected at the same time.

Bronchitis is a major problem in the older dog caused by a persistent infection or irritation, producing irreversible changes in the bronchi. A cough develops and increases until the dog seems to cough almost constantly.

Diseases producing laboured breathing

Laboured breathing is normally caused by those diseases which occupy space within the chest, and reduce the lung tissue available for oxygenation of the blood. An X-ray produces an accurate diagnosis.

- **Pneumonia**

This is an infection of the lungs. It can occur in the English Springer Spaniel and is caused by viruses, bacteria, fungi or inhaled matter, such as water.

■ **Chest tumours**

These can cause respiratory problems by occupying lung space and by causing the accumulation of fluid within the chest.

Accidents

Respiratory failure commonly follows accidents. Several types of injury may be seen:

■ **Haemorrhage into the lung**

Rupture of a blood vessel in the lung will release blood which fills the air sacs.

■ **Ruptured diaphragm**

This allows abdominal organs such as the liver, spleen or stomach to move forward into the chest cavity.

HEART AND CIRCULATION DISEASES

Heart attack in the human sense is uncommon. Collapse or fainting may occur due to inadequate cardiac function.

Heart murmurs

■ **Acquired disease**

This may result from wear and tear or from inflammation of heart valves, problems of rhythm and rate, or disease of the heart muscle.

Signs of disease may include weakness, lethargy, panting, cough, abdominal distension, collapse, and weight loss.

■ **Congenital heart disease**

This is usually due to valve defects or a hole

SECTION OF THE HEART

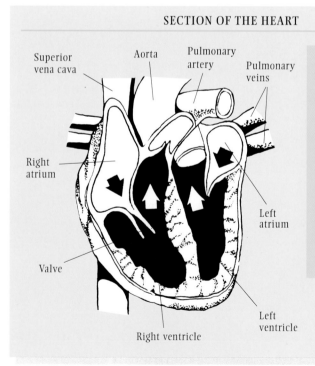

Superior vena cava

Aorta

Pulmonary artery

Pulmonary veins

Right atrium

Left atrium

Valve

Left ventricle

Right ventricle

The heart consists of two pairs of chambers: the atria and the ventricles. Deoxygenated blood enters the right atrium and is pumped out through the right ventricle to the lungs where it is oxygenated. This blood flows into the left atrium and thence through the left ventricle to the body's organs.

THE CIRCULATORY SYSTEM

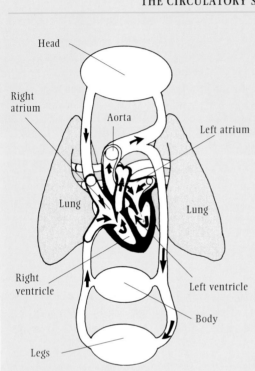

Head

Right atrium

Aorta

Left atrium

Lung

Lung

Right ventricle

Left ventricle

Body

Legs

Blood circulates around the dog's body by way of the circulatory system.

■ Oxygenated blood is pumped by the heart through the arteries to all the body organs, e.g. the brain, muscles and liver.

■ Oxygen and nutrients are extracted from the blood.

■ The used blood is returned by the veins to the right ventricle and then to the lungs.

■ In the lungs, carbon dioxide is exchanged for oxygen.

in the heart. Both are seen only rarely in the English Springer Spaniel.

Signs of disease may include the sudden death of a pup, or weakness and failure to thrive or grow at a normal rate.

■ **Congestive heart failure** is the end result of any of these defects.

Heart block

This is an acquired problem. A nerve impulse conduction failure occurs in the specialized heart muscle responsible for maintaining normal rhythm and rate.

SIGNS OF HEART FAILURE

These may include the following:
■ Exercise intolerance
■ Lethargy
■ Panting and/or coughing
■ Enlargement of the abdomen due to fluid accumulation
■ Poor digestion and weight loss

Veterinary investigation involves thorough examination, possibly X-rays of the chest, ECG, and, in some cases, ultrasound scanning.

Blood clotting defects

■ **Clotting problems** may result from poisoning with Warfarin rat poison. Haemorrhage then occurs which requires immediate treatment (see First Aid, page 133).

■ **Congenital clotting defects** arise if the pup is born with abnormal blood platelets or clotting factors, both of which are essential in normal clotting.

■ **von Willebrand's disease** is an inherited clotting disorder sometimes found in English Springer Spaniels.

Tumours

The spleen, which is a reservoir for blood, is a relatively common site for tumours, especially in older dogs. Splenic tumours can bleed slowly into the abdomen or rupture suddenly, causing collapse. Surgical removal of the spleen is necessary.

DIGESTIVE SYSTEM DISEASES

Mouth problems

Dental disease

■ **Dental tartar** forms on the tooth surfaces when left-over food (plaque) solidifies on the teeth. This irritates the adjacent gum, causing pain, mouth odour, gum recession, and ultimately tooth loss. This inevitable progression to periodontal disease may be prevented if plaque is removed by regular tooth brushing coupled with good diet, large chews and hard biscuits.

■ **Periodontal disease** or inflammation and erosion of the gums around the tooth roots is very common. It is a particularly common problem of the Springer Spaniel, probably because of saliva accumulation due to the lip folds. Careful scaling and polishing of the teeth by your vet under an anaesthetic is necessary to save the teeth.

■ **Dental caries** (tooth decay) is common in people, but not so in dogs *unless they are given chocolate.*

■ **Tooth fractures** can result from trauma in road accidents or if your dog is an enthusiastic stone catcher or chewer. A root treatment may be needed.

■ **Epulis** is a benign overgrowth of the gum. Surgical removal is needed.

Foreign bodies in the mouth

(See First Aid, page 138)

Salivary cysts

These may occur as swellings under the tongue or neck, resulting from a ruptured salivary duct. Surgical removal is usually necessary.

Mouth tumours

These are often highly malignant, growing rapidly and spreading to other organs. First

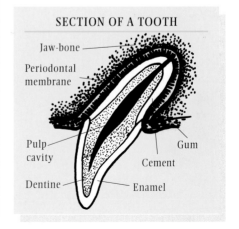

SECTION OF A TOOTH

Jaw-bone

Periodontal membrane

Pulp cavity

Gum

Cement

Dentine

Enamel

THE DIGESTIVE SYSTEM

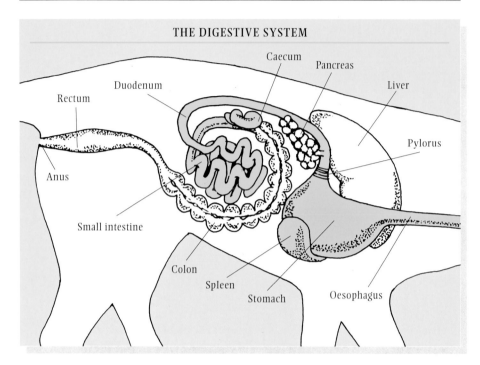

Caecum
Pancreas
Duodenum
Liver
Rectum
Pylorus
Anus
Small intestine
Colon
Spleen
Stomach
Oesophagus

symptoms may be bad breath, increased salivation, and bleeding from the mouth plus difficulties in eating.

Problems causing vomiting

■ **Gastritis**

This is inflammation of the stomach and can result from an unsuitable diet, scavenging or infection. The dog repeatedly vomits either food or yellowish fluid and froth, which may be blood stained.

■ **Obstruction of the oesophagus**

This leads to the regurgitation of food immediately after feeding, and may be caused by small bones or other foreign bodies. Diagnosis is confirmed either by X-ray or examination with an endoscope, and treatment must not be delayed.

■ **Obstruction lower down the gut, in the stomach or intestine**

This may result from items such as stones, corks etc. Tumours can also lead to obstructive vomiting. The dog rapidly becomes very ill and the diagnosis is usually confirmed by palpation, X-rays or exploratory surgery.

■ **Intussusception**

This is telescoping of the bowel which can follow diarrhoea, especially in puppies. Surgery is essential.

■ **Gastric dilation**

(See First Aid, page 139)

■ **Megoesophagus**

This is a defect in the wall of the oesophagus due to faulty nerve control, which leads to ballooning, retention of swallowed food and regurgitation before the food reaches the stomach.

PROBLEMS CAUSING DIARRHOEA

- **Dietary diarrhoea**
This can occur as a result of sudden changes in diet, scavenging, feeding unsuitable foods or stress (especially in pups when they go to their new home).
- **Pancreatic insufficiency**
(See below)
- **Enteritis**
This is inflammation of the small intestines which can be caused by infection, e.g. parvovirus, a severe worm burden or food poisoning. Continued diarrhoea leads to dehydration.
- **Colitis**
This is inflammation of the large bowel (colon). The symptoms include straining and frequent defaecation, watery faeces with mucous or blood, and often an otherwise healthy dog.
- **Tumours of the bowel**
Tumours of the bowel are more likely to cause vomiting than diarrhoea, but one which is called lymphosarcoma causes diffuse thickening of the gut lining which may lead to diarrhoea.

Pancreatic diseases

- **Acute pancreatitis**
This is an extremely painful and serious condition requiring intensive therapy. It can be life-threatening.
- **Pancreatic insufficiency**
Wasting of the cells of the pancreas which produce digestive enzymes leads to poor digestive function, persistent diarrhoea, weight loss and ravenous appetite. The condition, when it occurs, is often diagnosed in dogs of less than two years of age, and is occasionally seen in the English Springer Spaniel. Diagnosis is made on clinical symptoms and laboratory testing of blood and faeces.

- **Diabetes mellitus (Sugar diabetes)**
Another function of the pancreas is to manufacture the hormone insulin, which controls blood sugar levels. If insulin is deficient, blood and urine glucose levels rise, both of which can be detected on laboratory testing. Affected animals have an increased appetite and thirst, weight loss and lethargy. If left untreated, the dog may go into a diabetic coma.
- **Pancreatic tumours**
These are relatively common and are usually highly malignant. Symptoms vary from vomiting, weight loss and signs of abdominal pain to acute jaundice. The prognosis is usually hopeless, and death rapidly occurs.

LIVER DISEASES

- **Acute hepatitis** – infectious canine hepatitis and leptospirosis (see Infectious Diseases, page 108). This is not common as most dogs are vaccinated.
- **Chronic liver failure**
This can be due to heart failure, tumours or cirrhosis. Affected dogs usually lose weight and become depressed, off their food and may vomit. Diarrhoea and increased thirst are other possible symptoms. The liver may increase or decrease in size, and there is sometimes fluid retention in the abdomen. Jaundice is sometimes apparent. Diagnosis of liver disease depends on symptoms, blood tests, X-rays or ultrasound examination, and possibly liver biopsy.

SKIN DISEASES

Itchy skin diseases

Parasites

■ **Fleas** are the commonest cause of skin disease, and dogs often become allergic to them. They are dark, fast-moving, sideways-flattened insects, about two millimetres long. They spend about two hours a day feeding on the dog, then jump off and spend the rest of the day breeding and laying eggs. They live for about three weeks and can lay fifty eggs a day. Thus each flea may leave behind 1000 eggs which hatch out in as little as three weeks. It is important to treat the dog with an effective, modern veterinary product, and the environment, i.e. the house.

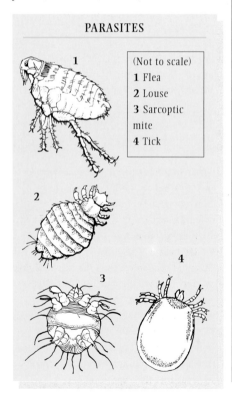

PARASITES

(Not to scale)
1 Flea
2 Louse
3 Sarcoptic mite
4 Tick

■ **Lice** are less common, but seem to enjoy life on Spaniels' long, floppy ears. They are small, whitish insects crawling very slowly between and up the hairs. They lay eggs on the hair, spend their entire life on the dog and are much easier to treat than fleas.

■ **Mange** is caused by mites (usually Sarcoptes) which burrow into the skin, causing intense irritation and hair loss. It is very contagious and more common in young dogs. Treatment is by anti-parasitic washes.

■ **Bacterial infections**
These are common in the dog and are often secondary to some other skin disease, such as mange or allergies. Long-term antibiotics are needed to control some skin diseases.

Pyoderma can be an acute, wet, painful area of the skin (wet eczema), or a more persistent infection appearing as ring-like sores. Both are seen in the English Springer Spaniel.

Furunculosis is a deeper, more serious infection seen quite often in the Springer Spaniel.

Lip fold dermatitis is a sore, foul-smelling infection of the fold of skin on each side of the lower jaw where the upper canine tooth lies. It is due to constant wetting of this skin by saliva and accumulated food particles. Antibiotic ointment will clear it temporarily, but surgical removal of this fold may be necessary. The Spaniels have a well-developed lip fold and are therefore very prone to this problem.

■ **Contact dermatitis**
This is an itchy reddening of the skin, usually of the abdomen, groin, armpit, or feet, where the hair is thinnest and less protective. It can be an allergic response to materials, such as wool, nylon or carpets, or to a direct irritant, such as oil, or a disinfectant.

■ **Lick granuloma**
This is a thickened, hairless patch of skin, usually seen on the front of the wrist or the

STRUCTURE OF THE SKIN

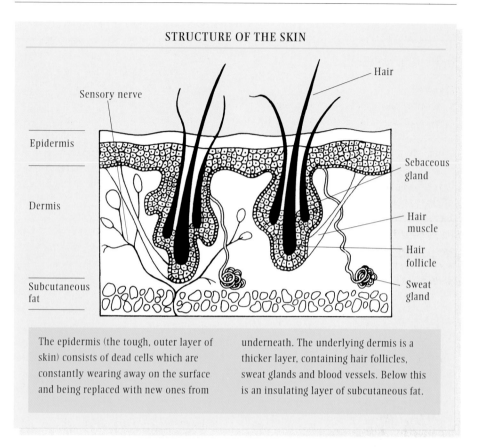

The epidermis (the tough, outer layer of skin) consists of dead cells which are constantly wearing away on the surface and being replaced with new ones from underneath. The underlying dermis is a thicker layer, containing hair follicles, sweat glands and blood vessels. Below this is an insulating layer of subcutaneous fat.

side of the ankle. It is thought to result from constant licking of this area because of boredom or neurosis.

Non-itchy skin diseases

■ Demodectic mange

Caused by a congenitally-transmitted parasitic mite, demodectic mange is seen usually in growing dogs, and causes non-itchy patchy hair loss. It is quite difficult to treat.

■ Ticks

These are parasitic spiders that attach themselves to the skin of the dog. They drop off after a week, when they resemble small grey peas, but should be removed when noticed. A tick can easily be removed by soaking it with surgical spirit and then pulling it out using fine tweezers.

■ Ringworm

This is a fungal infection of the hairs and skin causing bald patches. It is transmissible to people, especially children.

■ Hormonal skin disease

This patchy, symmetrical hair loss is not common in the Springer Spaniel, but spayed female Springers invariably develop a fluffy soft coat after their operation.

Tumours and cysts

- **Sebaceous cysts**

These are round, painless nodules in the skin and vary from 2 mm (¹/₈ in) up to 4 cm (1¹/₂ in) in diameter. They are seen in the Springer Spaniel, particularly as they get older.

- **Warts**

These are common in the older Springer Spaniel, and often develop in large numbers. Other skin tumours do occur.

- **Anal adenomas**

These frequently develop around the anus in un-neutered old male dogs. They ulcerate when they are quite small and produce small bleeding points.

DISEASES OF THE ANAL AREA

- **Anal sac impaction**

This is quite common in the Springer Spaniel, and is thought by some authorities to be linked with the tradition of docking the tail. The anal sacs are scent glands and little used in the dog. If the secretion accumulates in the gland instead of being emptied during defaecation as the dog raises his tail, the

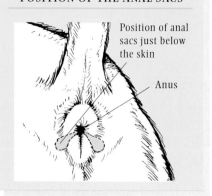

POSITION OF THE ANAL SACS

Position of anal sacs just below the skin

Anus

overful anal sac becomes itchy. The dog drags his anus along the ground or bites himself around the base of his tail. Unless the sacs are emptied by your vet, an abscess may form.

DISEASES OF THE FEET

- **Interdigital eczema**

Springers readily lick their feet after minor damage, and this makes the feet very wet. Infection then occurs between the pads.

- **Interdigital cysts and abscesses**

These are painful swellings between the toes which may make the dog lame. In most

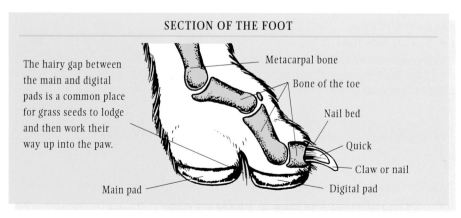

SECTION OF THE FOOT

The hairy gap between the main and digital pads is a common place for grass seeds to lodge and then work their way up into the paw.

Metacarpal bone

Bone of the toe

Nail bed

Quick

Claw or nail

Main pad

Digital pad

STRUCTURE OF THE FEET

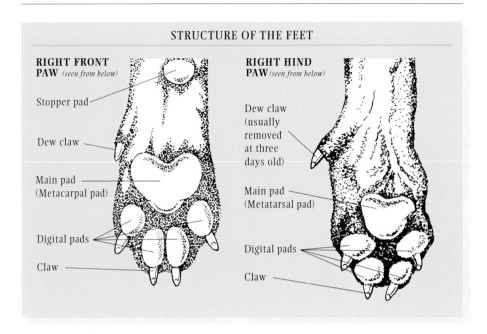

RIGHT FRONT PAW *(seen from below)*

Stopper pad

Dew claw

Main pad (Metacarpal pad)

Digital pads

Claw

RIGHT HIND PAW *(seen from below)*

Dew claw (usually removed at three days old)

Main pad (Metatarsal pad)

Digital pads

Claw

---

cases the cause is unknown, but in hairy-footed dogs like Springers, they can be caused by a grass seed penetrating the skin between the toes.

■ **Foreign body in the pad**

The most common foreign body is a sharp fragment of glass, or a thorn. The dog is usually very lame and the affected pad is painful to the touch. Often an entry point will be seen on the pad.

■ **Nail bed infections**

The toe becomes swollen and painful and the dog lame. The bone may become diseased and this can lead to amputation of the affected toe.

EAR DISEASES

Haematoma

This is a painless, sometimes large blood blister in the ear flap, usually caused by head shaking due to an ear infection or irritation. They do occur in the Springer Spaniel, and surgery is usually necessary.

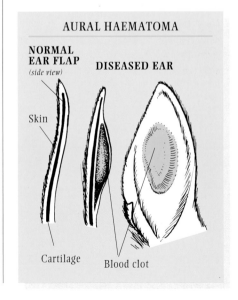

AURAL HAEMATOMA

NORMAL EAR FLAP *(side view)*

DISEASED EAR

Skin

Cartilage

Blood clot

Infection (otitis)

Due to his long, down-hanging and hairy ear flap, and consequent reduced ventilation of the ear, the Springer Spaniel is very prone to ear infections. When otitis occurs, a smelly discharge appears, and the dog shakes his head or scratches his ear. If the inner ear is affected, the dog may also show a head tilt or a disturbance in his balance.

■ **Treatment** with antibiotic ear drops is usually successful, but sometimes syringing or a surgical operation is needed. The vet must be consulted as there are several

GRASS SEED IN THE EAR

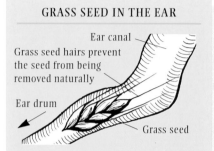

Ear canal

Grass seed hairs prevent the seed from being removed naturally

Ear drum

Grass seed

After becoming trapped, a grass seed can quickly work its way down the ear canal towards the ear drum.

STRUCTURE OF THE EAR

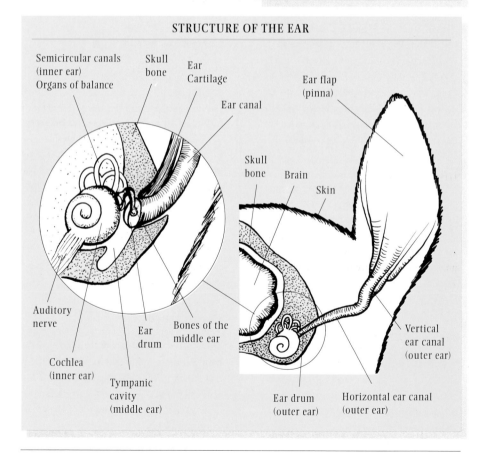

Semicircular canals (inner ear)
Organs of balance

Skull bone

Ear Cartilage

Ear canal

Ear flap (pinna)

Skull bone

Brain

Skin

Auditory nerve

Ear drum

Bones of the middle ear

Cochlea (inner ear)

Tympanic cavity (middle ear)

Vertical ear canal (outer ear)

Ear drum (outer ear)

Horizontal ear canal (outer ear)

possible reasons for ear disease including ear mites and grass seeds.

Foreign bodies

Because of their pendulous hairy ears, English Springer Spaniels are particularly prone to grass seeds entering the ear canal. If one finds its way into an ear, it can produce sudden severe distress and violent head shaking (see First Aid, page 138).

EYE DISEASES

Entropion

This is an inherited disease, usually of the young, growing dog, seen quite often in the Springer Spaniel. The edge of an eyelid rolls in so that the lashes rub against the surface of the eye, causing irritation of the eyeball. The eye is sore and wet with tears, and often kept closed. Surgical treatment is necessary.

Distichiasis

This condition is sometimes seen in the Springer Spaniel in which fine extra hairs grow along the edge of the eyelid and rub against the cornea. This leads to excessive tear production and the eye looks constantly wet. These hairs are removed temporarily by plucking, or permanently by surgery.

Conjunctivitis

This is common in the English Springer Spaniel. The white of the eye appears red and discharges. Possible causes include viruses, bacteria, chemicals, allergies, trauma or foreign bodies.

Keratitis

This is a very sore inflammation of the cornea which may appear blue and lose its shiny appearance.

Third eyelid disease

Prolapse of the Harderian gland, this is a small fleshy mass of tissue behind the third eyelid. In the Springer it can occasionally become displaced and protrude. Surgical removal is necessary.

Prolapse of the eye

(See First Aid, page 138)

Keratoconjunctivitis sicca (KCS) or Dry Eye

This is an autoimmune disease and is seen occasionally in the Springer Spaniel. It develops when the eye fails to produce tears. The cornea dries, keratitis develops, and the eye discharges a greyish, sticky mucus. In time, the cornea is invaded by blood vessels which cause pigmentation and loss of sight. One or both eyes can be affected. Medical treatment can control the disease in the early stages, but KCS can cause severe loss of vision and pain.

Corneal ulcer

This is an erosion of part of the surface of the cornea and can follow an injury or keratitis, and is very painful. The dog will hardly be able to open his eye which will flood tears. Veterinary treatment is essential in all cases of corneal ulcers.

Pannus

This is an autoimmune inflammation of the cornea. It occurs in some older Springers.

Glaucoma

This develops when the pressure of the fluid inside the eye increases. As the pressure increases, the eye becomes painful, inflamed, and excessive tear production occurs. There are two types of glaucoma – primary glaucoma, an inherited defect in some breeds, including the English Springer Spaniel, and secondary glaucoma which usually follows some trauma such as a dislocated lens.

Progressive retinal atrophy (PRA)

This is an inherited progressive degeneration of the retina of the eye, found in the Springer and other breeds, which may lead to total blindness. Affected dogs of either sex must not be used for breeding.

This disease is covered more fully under Special Problems of the English Springer Spaniel (see page 105).

Cataract

An opacity of the lens in one or both eyes. The pupil appears greyish instead of the normal black colour. In advanced cases the lens looks

THE EYE

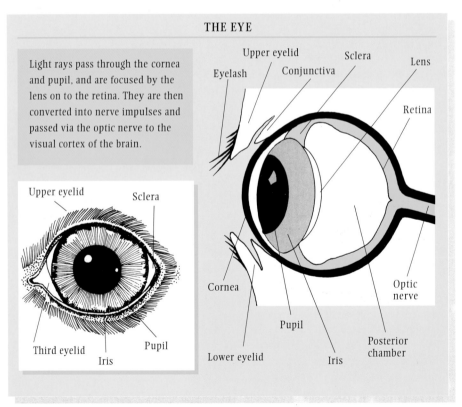

Light rays pass through the cornea and pupil, and are focused by the lens on to the retina. They are then converted into nerve impulses and passed via the optic nerve to the visual cortex of the brain.

Upper eyelid
Sclera
Eyelash
Conjunctiva
Lens
Sclera
Retina
Upper eyelid
Cornea
Optic nerve
Third eyelid
Pupil
Iris
Pupil
Lower eyelid
Iris
Posterior chamber

like a pearl and the dog may be blind. The causes of cataract in Springers include infection, diabetes mellitus, and trauma.

URINARY SYSTEM DISEASES

Diseases producing increased thirst

■ **Acute kidney failure**
The most common infectious agent producing acute nephritis is Leptospirosis (see Infectious Diseases, page 108).

■ **Chronic kidney failure**
This is common in old dogs and occurs when persistent damage to the kidney results in toxic substances starting to accumulate in the blood stream.

Diseases causing blood in the urine

■ **Cystitis**
This is an infection of the bladder. It is more common in the bitch because the infection has easy access through the shorter urethra. The clinical signs include increased frequency of urination, straining and sometimes a bloody urine. In all other respects the dog remains healthy.

■ **Urinary calculi or stones**
These can form in either the kidney or bladder.

■ **Kidney stones** are small kidney stones that can enter the ureters causing severe abdominal pain.

■ **Bladder stones**, or calculi, are fairly common in both sexes. In the bitch they are larger and straining is usually the only clinical sign. In the dog the most common sign is unproductive straining due to urinary obstruction. This is an emergency.

■ **Tumours of the bladder**
These occur and cause frequent straining and bloody urine, or, by occupying space within the bladder, cause incontinence.

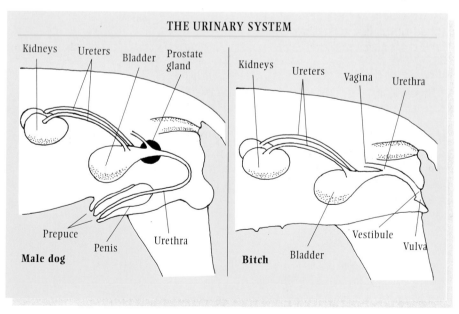

THE URINARY SYSTEM

Kidneys Ureters Bladder Prostate gland

Prepuce
Penis Urethra
Male dog

Kidneys Ureters Vagina Urethra

Vestibule
Vulva
Bitch Bladder

Incontinence

Occasionally, this occurs for no apparent reason, especially in the older bitch. Hormones or medicine to tighten the bladder sphincter can help.

REPRODUCTIVE ORGAN DISEASES

The male dog

■ **Retained testicle** (cryptorchidism)
Occasionally one or both testicles may fail to descend into the scrotum and remain somewhere along their developmental path. Surgery is advisable to remove retained testicles as they are very likely to develop cancer.

■ **Tumours**
These are fairly common but, fortunately, most are benign. One type of testicular tumour, known as a Sertoli cell tumour, produces female hormones leading to the development of female characteristics.

■ **Prostate disease**
This occurs in the older un-neutered Springer Spaniel, usually a benign enlargement where the prostate slowly increases in size. Hormone treatment or castration helps.

■ **Infection of the penis and sheath (balanitis)**
An increase and discolouration occurs in the discharge from the sheath, and the dog licks his penis more frequently.

■ **Paraphimosis**
Prolapse of the penis (see page 140).

■ **Castration**
This is of value in the treatment of some behavioural problems. Excessive sexual activity, such as mounting cushions or other

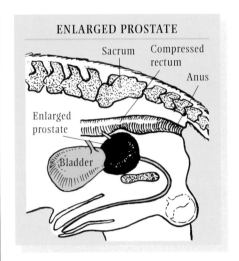

ENLARGED PROSTATE

Sacrum — Compressed rectum — Anus — Enlarged prostate — Bladder

dogs, and territorial urination may be eliminated by castration, as may certain types of aggression and the desire to escape and to wander.

The bitch

■ **Pyometra**
This is a common and serious disease of the older bitch although bitches which have had puppies seem less likely to develop it. The treatment of choice is usually an ovariohysterectomy.

■ **Mastitis**
This is an infection of the mammary glands and occurs usually in lactating bitches. The affected glands become swollen, hard and painful.

■ **Mammary tumours**
These are common in the older entire bitch. Most mammary tumours are benign, but where malignant, they can grow rapidly and spread to other organs. Early surgical removal of any lump is advisable because of the danger of malignancy.

False or pseudo-pregnancy

This occurs in most bitches about eight to twelve weeks after oestrus at the stage when the bitch would be lactating had she been pregnant. The signs vary and include poor appetite, lethargy, milk production, nest building, aggressiveness and attachment to a substitute puppy which is often a squeaky toy. Once a bitch has had a false pregnancy, she is likely to have one after each heat period.

- **Treatment,** if needed, is by hormones, and prevention is by a hormone injection, or course of tablets, and long term by an ovariohysterectomy.

Eclampsia

This is a very serious condition of the recently whelped bitch and can be fatal. The time of onset varies but it is usually seen when the pups are about three weeks old and making maximum demands on her. Her blood calcium level becomes too low due to the demands of the pups on her milk and she begins to show nervous symptoms. Initially she starts to twitch or shiver and appears unsteady, but this rapidly progresses to staggering, then convulsions. The vet must be contacted immediately as an injection of calcium is essential to save the life of the bitch.

Birth control

Hormone therapy

Several preparations, injections and tablets are available to prevent or postpone the bitch's heat period.

Spaying (ovariohysterectomy)

This is an operation to remove the uterus and ovaries, usually performed when the bitch is not on heat. Spaying is a good long-term solution to birth control in the bitch who will never breed.

THE REPRODUCTIVE SYSTEM

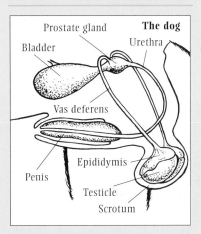

Sperm and testosterone are produced in the male dog's testicles. Sperm pass into the epididymis for storage, thence via the vas deferens during mating.

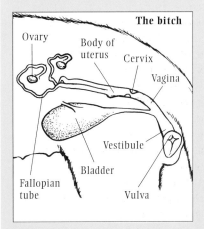

Eggs are produced in the ovaries and enter the uterus through the fallopian tubes. During the heat period, they can be fertilized by sperm.

NERVOUS SYSTEM DISEASES

The nervous system consists of two parts:

1 The central nervous system (CNS)
The brain and the spinal cord which runs in the vertebral column.

2 The peripheral nervous system
All the nerves which connect the CNS to the organs of the body.

- **Canine distemper virus**
(See Infectious Diseases, page 108)

- **Vestibular syndrome**
This is a fairly common condition of the older dog, and affects that part of the brain which controls balance. There is a sudden head tilt to the affected side, often flicking movements of the eyes called nystagmus, and the dog may fall or circle to that side. Many dogs will recover slowly but the condition may recur.

- **Slugbait (Metaldehyde) poisoning**
The dog appears 'drunk', uncoordinated, and may have convulsions. There is no specific treatment, but sedation may lead to recovery.

- **Epilepsy**
This is a nervous disorder causing fits. The dog has a sudden, unexpected fit or convulsion, which lasts for about two minutes. Recovery is fairly quick, although the dog may be dull and look confused for a few hours. Treatment is usually necessary and is successful as far as the control of epilepsy is concerned. Epilepsy appears to be more common in the Welsh Springer than the English Springer.

BONE, MUSCLE AND JOINT DISEASES

X-rays are necessary to confirm any diagnosis involving bone.

Bone infection (osteomyelitis)

This usually occurs after an injury such as a bite, or where a broken bone protrudes through the skin. Signs are pain, heat and swelling over the site, and if a limb bone is affected, there can be severe lameness.

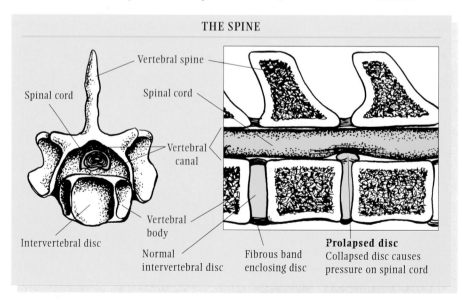

THE SPINE

Vertebral spine

Spinal cord

Spinal cord

Vertebral canal

Vertebral body

Intervertebral disc

Normal intervertebral disc

Fibrous band enclosing disc

Prolapsed disc
Collapsed disc causes pressure on spinal cord

TYPES OF FRACTURES

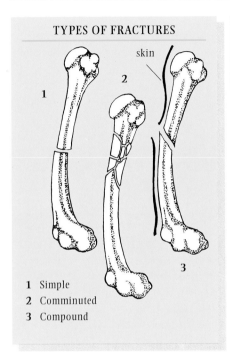

skin

1 Simple
2 Comminuted
3 Compound

CRUCIATE LIGAMENT RUPTURE

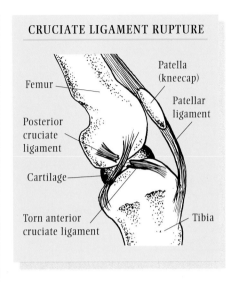

Femur
Posterior cruciate ligament
Cartilage
Torn anterior cruciate ligament
Patella (kneecap)
Patellar ligament
Tibia

■ **Fractures**
Any break or crack in a bone is called a
fracture. When a vet repairs a fracture, his aim
is to replace the fractured ends of bone into
their normal position and then to immobilize
the bone for four to six weeks. Depending on
the bone, and type of fracture, there are
several methods available – cage rest, external
casts, or surgery to perform internal fixation,
by, for example, plating or pinning.

■ **Bone tumours**
These are not common in the Springer Spaniel.

■ **Sprains**
A sprain is an inflammation of over-stretched
joint ligaments. The joint is hot, swollen and
painful, and the dog is lame.

■ **Cruciate ligament rupture**
When these rupture, as a result of a severe
sprain, the stifle or knee joint is destabilized
and the dog becomes instantly and severely
lame on that leg. This often occurs in middle-
aged, overweight Springers. Surgical repair is
usually necessary.

■ **Arthritis or degenerative joint disease**
This occurs in the Springer Spaniel. It results
in thickening of the joint capsule, formation
of abnormal new bone around the edges of the
joint and, sometimes, wearing of the joint
cartilage. The joint becomes enlarged and

TYPICAL NORMAL JOINT

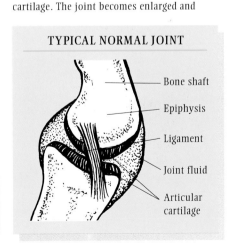

Bone shaft
Epiphysis
Ligament
Joint fluid
Articular cartilage

THE SKELETON

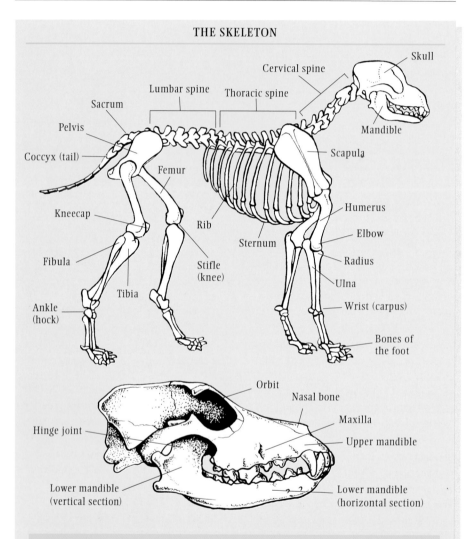

Skull

Cervical spine

Lumbar spine   Thoracic spine

Sacrum

Pelvis

Mandible

Coccyx (tail)

Scapula

Femur

Humerus

Kneecap

Elbow

Rib

Sternum

Radius

Fibula

Stifle (knee)

Ulna

Tibia

Ankle (hock)

Wrist (carpus)

Bones of the foot

Orbit

Nasal bone

Maxilla

Hinge joint

Upper mandible

Lower mandible (vertical section)

Lower mandible (horizontal section)

The skeleton is the framework for the body. All the dog's ligaments, muscles and tendons are attached to the bones, 319 of them in total. By a process called ossification, cartilage template is calcified to produce bone. Bones are living tissue and they respond to the stresses and strains placed upon them. To build and keep healthy bones, dogs need a nutritionally balanced diet which contains an adequate supply of calcium, vitamin D and phosphorus.

painful, and has a reduced range of movement. It tends to occur in the older dog and usually affects the hips, stifles (knees) and elbows.

- **Spondylitis**

This is arthritis of the spine. This is not common in the Springer Spaniel.

Hip dysplasia (HD)

Hip dysplasia does occur in the Springer Spaniel and is a serious developmental abnormality. In a normal dog the hip is a 'ball and socket' joint and allows a wide range of movement. The rounded end at the top of the femur, the femoral head, fits tightly into the acetabulum in the pelvis, a deep, cup-shaped socket. Hip dysplasia is the development instead of a shallow acetabulum, an irregular, distorted head of the femur, and slackness of the joint ligaments. Excessive movement can and does occur between the femur and the pelvis, and this leads to a malfunctioning, painful joint which will gradually become arthritic.

- **Causes of hip dysplasia**

It is known to be inherited but there are other factors involved, such as poor nutrition, too much exercise, or even being overweight during the rapid growth phase of the young dog.

- **Early signs of hip dysplasia in puppies**

A puppy developing severe hip dysplasia may have great difficulty walking, and particularly standing up from a sitting position which he may find painful and cry out. He may appear to sway when running, or characteristically use both hind legs together in a bunny hop. These signs may be present as young as five months old. Mildly affected puppies may show no signs at all at this stage, but at about eight years of age begin to develop arthritis.

- **Confirming hip dysplasia**

Your vet will suspect hip dysplasia in a

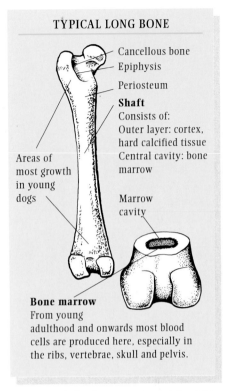

TYPICAL LONG BONE

Cancellous bone
Epiphysis
Periosteum
Shaft
Consists of:
Outer layer: cortex, hard calcified tissue
Central cavity: bone marrow

Areas of most growth in young dogs

Marrow cavity

Bone marrow
From young adulthood and onwards most blood cells are produced here, especially in the ribs, vertebrae, skull and pelvis.

Springer with the above symptoms at the right age. Confirmation is by manipulation of the suspect joint and by an X-ray. This should be carried out under general anaesthetic for safety reasons for the operator, and for correct positioning of the dog.

- **Hip dysplasia scheme**

All Springers, of both sexes, intended for breeding should be X-rayed at not less than one year of age. The British Veterinary Association and the Kennel Club have for many years run a joint scheme (the BVA/KC hip dysplasia scheme) based on hip scoring, and the vet submits the X-ray, bearing the KC registration number of the dog, to the scheme. Each hip is scored from 0 to 54, making a total of 108 maximum between the two hips.

The lower the score the better, and 0:0 is the best score possible.

At the time of going to print, only 336 X-rays have been submitted for scrutiny and the average combined score for the English Springer Spaniel so far is 13. No-one should breed from a dog or bitch with a higher hip score than the average for the breed if HD is ever to be reduced or eliminated from that breed. Anyone buying a puppy should ensure both parents have been X-rayed, scored, and achieved a low score. This is not, of course, an absolute guarantee that the puppy will not eventually develop hip dysplasia, but it

should considerably reduce the chances.

■ **Treatment** If the hip dysplasia is diagnosed at an early stage, and is mild, a combination of anabolic steroids, restricted exercise, and a keeping your dog slightly underweight during the growth phase will often lead to a sound adult dog. He may, however, only be able to indulge in a limited amount of exercise during his life. Too much at this stage may lead to arthritis later. In more severe cases, one of several available surgical techniques will be needed, but the dog will never be as agile as an unaffected dog.

HIP DYSPLASIA

NORMAL HIP JOINT

Head of femur

Neck

Acetabulum

Pelvis

Femur

This normal hip would score 0 on the BVA/KC hip dysplasia scheme.

HIP DYSPLASIA

Enlarged joint space

Shallow socket

Flattened head

Femur   Thickened neck

This abnormal hip would score approximately 26 on the BVA/KC hip dysplasia scheme giving a total score of 52 if the other hip was similarly deformed.

CHAPTER NINE

FIRST AID, ACCIDENTS AND EMERGENCIES

First Aid is the emergency care given to a dog suffering injury or illness of sudden onset.

AIMS OF FIRST AID

1 Keep the dog alive.
2 Prevent unnecessary suffering.
3 Prevent further injury.

RULES OF FIRST AID

1

Keep calm. If you panic you will be unable to help effectively.

2

Contact a vet as soon as possible. Advice given over the telephone may be life-saving.

3

Avoid injury to yourself. A distressed or injured animal may bite so use a muzzle if necessary (see muzzling, page 140).

4

Control haemorrhage. Excessive blood loss can lead to severe shock and death (see haemorrhage, page 133).

5

Maintain an airway. Failure to breathe or obtain adequate oxygen can lead to brain damage or loss of life within five minutes (see airway obstruction and artificial respiration, page 131).

COMMON ACCIDENTS AND EMERGENCIES

The following common accidents and emergencies all require First Aid action. In an emergency, your priorities are to keep the dog alive and comfortable until he can be examined by a vet. In many cases, there is effective action that you can take immediately to help preserve your dog's health and life.

SHOCK AND ROAD ACCIDENTS

SHOCK

This is a serious clinical syndrome which can cause death. Shock can follow road accidents, severe burns, electrocution, extremes of heat and cold, heart failure, poisoning, severe fluid loss, reactions to drugs, insect stings or snake bite.

SIGNS OF SHOCK
- Weakness or collapse
- Pale gums
- Cold extremities, e.g. feet and ears
- Weak pulse and rapid heart
- Rapid, shallow breathing

RECOMMENDED ACTION

1 Act immediately. Give cardiac massage (see page 132) and/or artificial respiration (see page 131) if necessary, after checking for a clear airway.

2 Keep the dog flat and warm. Control external haemorrhage (page 133).

3 Veterinary treatment is essential thereafter.

ROAD ACCIDENTS

Injuries resulting from a fast-moving vehicle colliding with an animal can be very serious. Road accidents may result in:
- Death
- Head injuries
- Spinal damage
- Internal haemorrhage, bruising and rupture of major organs, e.g. liver, spleen, kidneys
- Fractured ribs and lung damage, possibly resulting in haemothorax (blood in the chest cavity) or pneumothorax (air in the chest cavity)
- Fractured limbs with or without nerve damage
- External haemorrhage, wounds, tears and bruising

RECOMMENDED ACTION

1 Assess the situation and move the dog to a safe position. Use a blanket to transport him and keep him flat.

2 Check for signs of life: feel for a heart beat (see cardiac massage, page 132), and watch for the rise and fall of the chest wall.

3 If the dog is breathing, treat as for shock (see above). If he is not breathing but there is a heart beat, give artificial respiration, after checking for airway obstruction. Consider the use of a muzzle (see muzzling, page 140).

4 Control external haemorrhage (see haemorrhage, page 133).

5 Keep the dog warm and flat at all times, and seek veterinary help.

AIRWAY OBSTRUCTION

■ **FOREIGN BODY IN THE THROAT,** e.g. a ball.

■ **FOLLOWING A ROAD ACCIDENT**, or convulsion, blood, saliva or vomit in the throat may obstruct breathing.

RECOMMENDED ACTION

1

This is an acute emergency. Do not try to pull out the object. Push it upwards and forwards from behind the throat so that it moves from its position where it is obstructing the larynx, into the mouth.

2

The dog should now be able to breathe. Remove the object from his mouth.

RECOMMENDED ACTION

1

Pull the tongue forwards and clear any obstruction with your fingers.

2

Then, with the dog on his side, extend the head and neck forwards to maintain a clear airway.

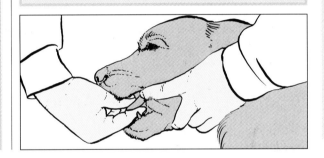

DROWNING

RECOMMENDED ACTION

1

Out of water, remove the collar and place the dog on his side with his head lower than his body.

2

With hands, apply firm downward pressure on chest at five-second intervals.

ARTIFICIAL RESPIRATION

This is the method for helping a dog which has a clear airway but cannot breathe.

RECOMMENDED ACTION

Use mouth-to-mouth resuscitation by cupping your hands over his nose and mouth and blowing into his nostrils every five seconds.

SHOCK AND ROAD ACCIDENTS

CARDIAC MASSAGE

This is required if your dog's heart fails.

RECOMMENDED ACTION

1

With the dog lying on his right side, feel for a heart beat with your fingers on the chest wall behind the dog's elbows on his left side.

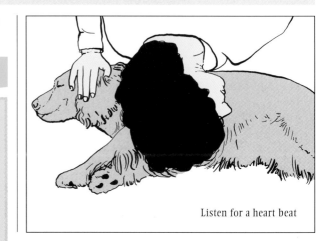

Listen for a heart beat

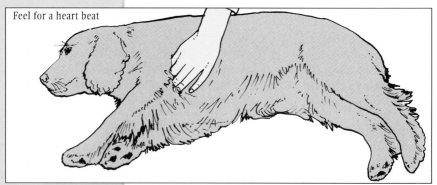

Feel for a heart beat

2

If you feel nothing, squeeze rhythmically with your palms, placing one hand on top of the other, as shown, at two-second intervals, pressing down hard.

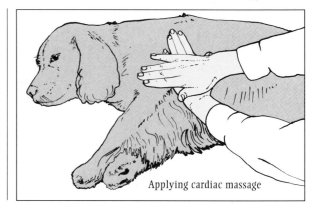

Applying cardiac massage

Haemorrhage

Severe haemorrhage must be controlled, as it leads to a precipitous fall in blood pressure and the onset of shock. Haemorrhage is likely to result from deep surface wounds, or internal injuries, e.g. following a road accident.

- **FOR SURFACE WOUNDS**

Locate the bleeding point and apply pressure either with:
- **Your thumb** or
- **A pressure bandage** (preferred method) or
- **A tourniquet**

1 **Pressure bandage** Use a pad of gauze, cotton wool or cloth against the wound and tightly bandage around it. In the

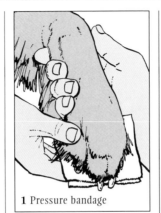

1 Pressure bandage

absence of a proper dressing, use a clean handkerchief or scarf.

2 If the bleeding continues, apply another dressing on top of the first.

1 **Tourniquet** (on limbs and tail) Tie a narrow piece of cloth, a neck tie or dog lead tightly

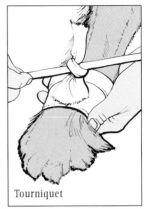

Tourniquet

around the limb, nearer to the body than the wound itself.

2 Using a pencil or stick within the knot, twist until it becomes tight enough to stop the blood flow.

3 **Important**: you must seek veterinary assistance as soon as possible.

Note: Tourniquets should be applied for no longer than fifteen minutes at a time, or tissue death may result.

- **FOR INTERNAL BLEEDING**

1 You should keep the animal quiet and warm, and minimize any movement.

2 **Important**: you must seek veterinary assistance as soon as possible.

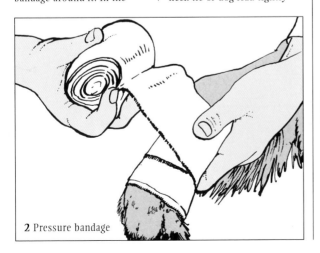

2 Pressure bandage

WOUNDS

These may result from road accidents, dog fights, sharp stones or glass, etc. Deep wounds may cause serious bleeding, bone or nerve damage.

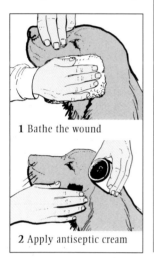

1 Bathe the wound

2 Apply antiseptic cream

RECOMMENDED ACTION

1 Deal with external bleeding (see haemorrhage, page 133) and keep the dog quiet before seeking veterinary attention.

2 Cut feet or pads should be bandaged to prevent further blood loss.

3 Minor cuts, abrasions and bruising should be bathed with warm salt solution (one

5ml teaspoonful per 550ml (1 pint) of water). They should be protected from further injury or contamination. Apply some antiseptic cream, if necessary.

4 If in doubt, ask your vet to check in case the wound needs suturing or antibiotic therapy, particularly if caused by fighting. Even minor cuts and punctures can be complicated by the presence of a foreign body.

FRACTURES

Broken bones, especially in the legs, often result from road accidents. Be careful when lifting and transporting the affected dog.

■ **LEG FRACTURES**

RECOMMENDED ACTION

1 Broken lower leg bones can sometimes be straightened gently, bandaged and then taped or tied with string to a make-

shift splint, e.g. a piece of wood or rolled-up newspaper or cardboard.

2 Otherwise, support the leg to prevent any movement. Take the dog to the vet immediately.

■ **OTHER FRACTURES**
These may be more difficult to diagnose. If you suspect a fracture, transport your dog very gently and with great care, and get him to the vet.

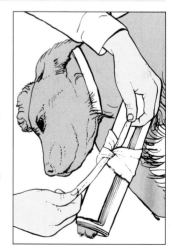

OTHER ACCIDENTS AND EMERGENCIES

COLLAPSE

This may be accompanied by loss of consciousness, but not in every case.

POSSIBLE CAUSES
- Head trauma, e.g. following a road accident
- Heart failure
- Stroke
- Hyperthermia (heat stroke)
- Hypothermia (cold)
- Hypocalcaemia (low calcium)
- Shock
- Spinal fractures
- Asphyxia (interference with breathing)
- Electrocution
- Poisoning

Note: you should refer to the relevant section for further details of these problems.

RECOMMENDED ACTION

1 The collapsed animal must be moved with care to avoid further damage.

2 Gently slide him on his side onto a blanket or coat.

3 Check he is breathing, and then keep him quiet and warm until you obtain professional help.

4 If he is not breathing, administer artificial respiration immediately, after checking for a clear airway (see page 131).

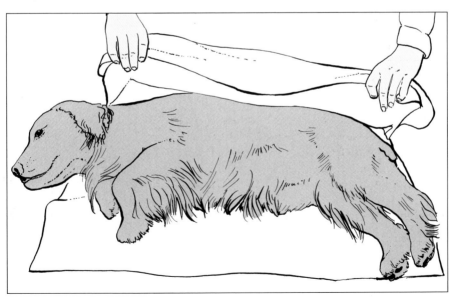

OTHER ACCIDENTS AND EMERGENCIES

CONVULSIONS (FITS OR SEIZURES)

These are very alarming to dog owners. Uncontrolled spasms, 'paddling' of legs, loss of consciousness, sometimes salivation and involuntary urination or defecation occur. Most convulsions only last a few minutes, but the dog is often confused and dazed afterwards.

POSSIBLE CAUSES

- Poisoning
- Head injuries
- Brain tumours
- Liver and kidney disease
- Meningitis
- Epilepsy
- Low blood glucose, e.g. in diabetes, or low blood calcium, e.g. in eclampsia

RECOMMENDED ACTION

1 Unless he is in a dangerous situation, do not attempt to hold the dog, but protect him from damaging himself.

2 Do not give him anything by mouth.

3 Try to keep him quiet, cool and, if possible, in a darkened room until he sees the vet.

4 If you have to move your English Springer Spaniel, cover him with a blanket first.

HEART FAILURE

This is not as common in dogs as in humans. Affected dogs faint, usually during exercise, and lose consciousness. The mucous membranes appear pale or slightly blue.

RECOMMENDED ACTION

1 Cover the dog in a blanket, and lie him on his side.

2 Massage his chest behind the elbows (see cardiac massage, page 132).

3 When he recovers, take him straight to the vet.

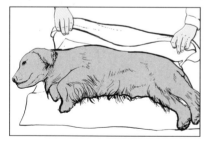

1 An affected dog should be covered with a blanket and laid on his side.
2 Apply cardiac massage, pressing down firmly at two-second intervals.

HEAT-STROKE

This occurs in hot weather, especially when dogs have been left in cars with insufficient ventilation. Affected animals are extremely distressed, panting and possibly collapsed. They can die rapidly. A heat-stroke case should be treated as an acute emergency.

RECOMMENDED ACTION

1 Either place the dog in a cold bath or run cold water over his body until his temperature is in the normal range.

2 Offer water with added salt (one 5ml teaspoonful per half litre/1pint water).

3 Treatment for shock may be necessary (see page 130).

ELECTROCUTION

This is most likely to occur in a bored puppy who chews through a cable. Electrocution may kill him outright or lead to delayed shock.

■ **DO NOT TOUCH HIM BEFORE YOU SWITCH OFF THE ELECTRICITY SOURCE.**

RECOMMENDED ACTION

1 If he is not breathing, begin artificial respiration immediately (see page 131) and keep him warm.

2 Contact your vet; if he survives he will need treatment for shock (see page 130).

BURNS AND SCALDS

POSSIBLE CAUSES
■ Spilled hot drinks, boiling water or fat.
■ Friction, chemical and electrical burns.

RECOMMENDED ACTION

1 Immediately apply running cold water and, thereafter, cold compresses, ice packs or packets of frozen peas to the affected area.

2 Veterinary attention is essential in most cases.

SNAKE BITE

Outdoor-loving dogs can be bitten by the adder in Great Britain. Signs are pain accompanied by a soft swelling around two puncture wounds, usually on the head, neck or limbs. Trembling, collapse, shock and even death can ensue.

RECOMMENDED ACTION

1 Do not let the dog walk; carry him to the car.

2 Keep him warm, and take him immediately to the vet.

OTHER ACCIDENTS AND EMERGENCIES

FOREIGN BODIES

■ **IN THE MOUTH**
Sticks or bones wedged between the teeth cause frantic pawing at the mouth and salivation.

RECOMMENDED ACTION

Remove the foreign body with your fingers or pliers, using a wooden block placed between the dog's canine teeth if possible to aid the safety of this procedure. Some objects have to be removed under general anaesthesia.
Note: a ball in the throat is dealt with in airway obstruction (see page 131), and is a critical emergency.

■ **FISH HOOKS**
Never try to pull these out, wherever they are.

RECOMMENDED ACTION

Push the fish hook through the skin, cut the line end off with pliers, and then pull it out.

■ **IN THE EAR – GRASS SEEDS**
These are the little spiky seeds of the wild barley, and are a real nuisance to Springer Spaniels with their long, floppy ears, and long coat. If one finds its way into an ear, it can produce sudden severe distress and violent head shaking.

RECOMMENDED ACTION

If you can see the grass seed, gently but firmly pull it out with a pair of tweezers, and check that it is intact. If you cannot see it, or feel that you may have left some in, you should call the vet immediately.

■ **IN THE FOOT**
Glass, thorns or splinters can penetrate the pads or soft skin, causing pain, and infection if neglected.

RECOMMENDED ACTION

Soak the foot in warm salt water and then use a sharp sterilized needle or pair of tweezers to extract the foreign body. If this is not possible, take your dog to the vet who will remove it under local or general anaesthetic if necessary.

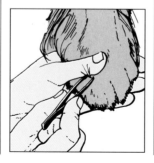

NOSE BLEEDS

These may be caused by trauma or violent sneezing, but are also related in some cases to ulceration of the lining of the nasal cavity.

RECOMMENDED ACTION

1 Keep the dog quiet and use ice packs on the nose.

2 Contact your vet if the bleeding persists.

EYEBALL PROLAPSE

Not a common problem in English Springer Spaniels, but may arise from head trauma, e.g. following a dog fight. The eye is forced out of its socket and sight is lost unless it is replaced within fifteen minutes.

RECOMMENDED ACTION

1 Speed is essential. One person should pull the eyelids apart while the other gently presses the eyeball back into its socket, using moist sterile gauze or cloth.

2 If this is impossible, cover the eye with moist sterile gauze and take the dog to your vet immediately.

GASTRIC DILATION

This is an emergency and cannot be treated at home. The stomach distends with gas and froth which the dog cannot easily eliminate. In some cases, the stomach then rotates and a torsion occurs, so the gases cannot escape at all and the stomach rapidly fills the abdomen. This causes pain, respiratory distress and circulatory failure. Life-threatening shock follows. It is a very rare condition in the English Springer Spaniel.

PREVENTIVE ACTION

1 Avoid the problem by not exercising your dog vigorously for two hours after a full meal.

2 If your dog is becoming bloated and has difficulty breathing, he is unlikely to survive unless he has veterinary attention within half an hour of the onset of symptoms, so get him to the vet immediately.

POISONING

Dogs can be poisoned by pesticides, herbicides, poisonous plants, paints, antifreeze or an overdose of drugs (animal or human).

■ If poisoning is suspected, first try to determine the agent involved, and find out if it is corrosive or not. This may be indicated on the container, but may also be evident from the blistering of the lips, gums and tongue, and increased salivation.

RECOMMENDED ACTION

■ **CORROSIVE POISONS**

1 Wash the inside of the dog's mouth.

2 Give him milk and bread to protect the gut against the effects of the corrosive.

3 Seek veterinary help.

■ **OTHER POISONS**

1 If the dog is conscious, make him vomit within half an hour of taking the poison.

2 A crystal of washing soda or a few 15ml tablespoonfuls of strong salt solution can be given carefully by mouth.

3 Retain a sample of vomit to aid identification of the poison, or take the poison container with you to show the vet. There may be a specific antidote, and any information can help in treatment.

STINGS

Bee and wasp stings often occur around the head, front limbs or mouth. The dog usually shows sudden pain and paws at, or licks, the stung area. A soft, painful swelling appears; sometimes the dog seems unwell or lethargic. Stings in the mouth and throat can be distressing and dangerous.

RECOMMENDED ACTION

1 Withdraw the sting (bees).

2 Then you can bathe the area in:

■ Vinegar for wasps

■ Bicarbonate for bees

3 An antihistamine injection may be needed.

OTHER ACCIDENTS AND EMERGENCIES

BREEDING

■ **ECLAMPSIA**

This is a very serious condition of the recently whelped bitch and can be fatal. Initially she starts to twitch and appears unsteady. This progresses to staggering, then convulsions.

RECOMMENDED ACTION

Contact the vet immediately as an injection of calcium is essential to save her life. Keep her warm and, if you have any, administer calcium colloidal suspension or a calcium tablet in the meantime.

■ **PARAPHIMOSIS**

This problem may occur after mating, in the male. The engorged penis is unable to retract into the sheath.

RECOMMENDED ACTION

The exposed penis should be bathed in cool, sterile water to reduce its size. Lubricate with petroleum jelly or soap to pull the sheath forward. If correction is impossible, ring the vet.

MUZZLING

This will allow a nervous, distressed or injured dog to be examined safely, without the risk of being bitten. A tape or bandage is secured around the muzzle as illustrated. However, a muzzle should not be applied in the following circumstances:

■ Airway obstruction

■ Loss of consciousness

■ Compromised breathing or severe chest injury

1   Tie a knot in the bandage.

2   Wrap around the dog's muzzle with the knot under the lower jaw and tie on top of the muzzle.

3   Cross the ends under the jaw and tie firmly behind the dog's head.

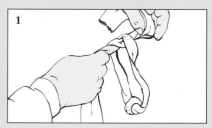

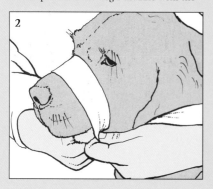

GLOSSARY

Angulation
The angles created by bones meeting at a joint.

Breed standard
The description laid down by the Kennel Club of the perfect breed specimen.

Brood bitch
A female dog which is used for breeding.

Carpals
These are the wrist bones.

Croup
This is the dog's rump: the front of the pelvis to the start of the tail.

Dam
The mother of puppies.

Dew claw
A fifth toe above the ground on the inside of the legs.

Elbow
The joint at the top of the forearm below the upper arm.

Flank
The area between the last rib and hip on the side of the body.

Furnishings
The long hair on the head, legs, thighs, back of buttocks or tail.

Gait
How a dog moves at different speeds.

Guard hairs
Long hairs that grow through the undercoat.

Muzzle
The foreface, or front of the head.

Occiput
The back upper part of the skull.

Oestrus
The periods when a bitch is 'on heat' or 'in season' and responsive to mating.

Pastern
Between the wrist (carpus) and the digits of the forelegs.

Scissor bite
Strong jaws with upper teeth overlapping lower ones.

Stifle
The hind leg joint, or 'knee'.

Undercoat
A dense, short coat hidden below the top-coat.

Whelping
The act of giving birth.

Whelps
Puppies that have not been weaned.

Whiskers
Long hairs on the jaw and muzzle.

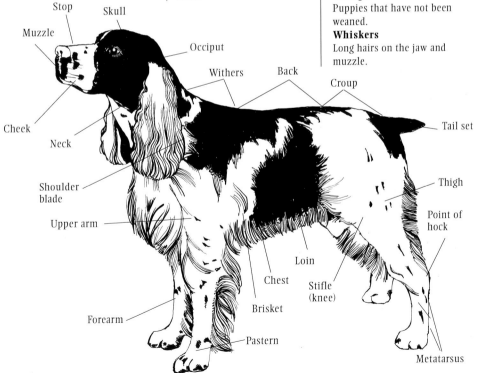

INDEX

USEFUL ADDRESSES

Animal Aunts
Wydnooch
45 Fairview Rd
Headley Down
Hampshire
GU38 8HQ
(Home sitters,
holidays)

**Animal Studies
Centre**
Waltham-on-the-Wolds
Melton Mowbray
Leics LE14 4RS
(Animal nutrition)

**Association of Pet
Behaviour
Counsellors**
257 Royal College St.
London
NW1 9LU

**British Veterinary
Association**
7 Mansfield Street
London W1M 0AT

**Dog Breeders
Insurance Co Ltd**
9 St Stephens Court
St Stephens Road

Bournemouth
BH2 6LG
(Books of cover notes
for dog breeders)

**Featherbed
Country Club**
High Wycombe
Bucks
(Luxury dog
accommodation)

**Guide Dogs for the
Blind Association**
Hillfield
Burghfield
Reading
RG7 3YG

**Hearing Dogs for
the Deaf**
The Training Centre
London Road
Lewknor
Oxon OX9 5RY

Home Sitters
Buckland Wharf
Buckland
Aylesbury
Bucks
HP22 5LO

The Kennel Club
1-5 Clarges Street
Piccadilly
London
W1Y 8AB
(Breed Standards,
Breed Club and Field
Trial contact
addresses, registration
forms, Good Citizen
training scheme)

**National Canine
Defence League**
1 & 2 Pratt Mews
London
NW1 0AD

Pet Plan Insurance
Westcross House
2 Westcross Way
Brentwood
Middlesex
TW8 9YP

**Pets As Therapy
(PAT Dogs)**
6 New Road
Ditton
Kent
ME20 6AD
(Information: how

friendly dogs can
join the hospital
visiting scheme)

**PRO Dogs National
Charity**
4 New Road
Ditton
Kent
ME20 6AD
(Information: Better
British Breeders,
worming certificates
to provide with
puppies, how to cope
with grief on the loss
of a loved dog etc.)

**Royal Society for
the Prevention of
Cruelty to Animals**
RSPCA Headquarters
Causeway
Horsham
West Sussex
RH12 1HG

SCAMPERS SCHOOL FOR DOGS

Scampers helps to train over 200 dogs and puppies every week, using kind, reward-based methods and behaviour therapy, in its unique indoor training facilities. Expert advice is given on all aspects of dog care, and there are puppy, beginners, intermediate and advanced classes. Scampers also run courses for other dog trainers and people interested in a career in dog training.

Scampers Pet Products

This specialist mail order service provides special products, including books, videos, toys, accessories and training equipment, for dog owners. It is based

at Scampers Petcare Superstore, which offers one of the largest ranges of dog accessories in the UK. For more information on Scampers School for Dogs, Scampers Petcare Superstore or Scampers Pet Products contact:

Scampers Petcare Superstore
Northfield Road
Soham
Nr. Ely
Cambs CB7 5UF
Tel: 01353 720431
Fax: 01353 624202